AFTER SHOCKS

AFTER SHOCKS

The Poetry of Recovery
for Life-Shattering Events

Edited by
Tom Lombardo

Sante Lucia Books
Atlanta, Georgia

Sante Lucia Books
Suite 500
1401 Peachtree St.N.E.
Atlanta, GA 30309

First Edition

Cover design by Kevin Watson & Tom Lombardo

Tom Lombardo photo by Lucia Lombardo

Printed on acid-free paper

ISBN 978-0-9816354-0-8

for Hope

Contents

Recovery From Death of a Spouse

Recovery From War

Recovery From Exile

Recovery From Abuse

Recovery From Divorce or Loss of Lover

Recovery From Loss of Innocence

Recovery From Illness or Injury

Recovery From Death of Family or Friends

Recovery From Stresses of Living

These Lives We Live

by Afaa Michael Weaver

After Shocks: The Poetry of Recovery for Life-Shattering Events reminds us of
our ability to become whole again, to reclaim ourselves after disaster has
entered our lives. At some point, we confront the prospect that life is
about love and loss, and the complexities that give meaning to love and
loss. It seems the human heart is in a constant struggle to negotiate this
rugged landscape.

While thinking of what to say about this wonderful and important
anthology, I was reminded that I am writing in the fortieth anniversary
year of the assassination of The Rev. Dr. Martin Luther King Jr. In the
brief moment it took to take his life, those closest to him were in shock
as he lay in the arms of his comrade, Ralph Abernathy, bidding a wordless
goodbye to the world he tried so hard to change, and the trauma of his
death sent tremors through America's accumulated trauma, its complex
history to show us once again how trauma, the shock of it and the long
trajectory of recovery, connects us all as human beings. Dr. King sought
to lead us toward a recovery from our truncated realities, from the
misshapen way the country has formed itself from its traumatic past,
and we are still in recovery from our loss of his presence in our lives.
So his life is a lesson in what this anthology takes as its central subject,
recovery.

Taking this idea of recovery in its general sense, the anthology adds
several categories across the broad spectrum of trauma to the familiar
category of substance abuse. The richness of such a collection is rooted
in its many possible realizations for the reader, one of which is that traumas
are often related. Abuse can manifest in addictions, and addictions can
lead to a network of unstable relationships that lay open the possibilities
for more loss. It is here we have also the chance to see how deeply human
we are, if we take being human the quality of being fallible. We experience

loss and trouble sometimes in a network of events that seem to be an awful falling of the dominoes.

In "Midwinter Letter," Donald Hall writes

> I lean forward from emptiness
> eager for more emptiness...
> Remembered happiness is agony;
> so is remembered agony.

There is this sense of emptiness as what we are left with after loss, whether that loss be a loved one, our innocence, or all the other precious things that spell wholeness, and then there is the emptiness of no longer grieving. So the poet speaks out of the midst of this process of putting the pieces of our lives together after a loved one has departed, as that is the specific subject here. However, this anthology shows us the process applies to trauma generally. It is the gut of mourning.

It is left to the poets to walk through the aftermath of loss, counting the broken things inside us, and to walk through the loss as it is happening, making the notes in the quick space between thought and language where only the poet can live. In this collection poets show themselves as guardians. In "Wartime (*Háború*)," Sándor Kányádi notes the bustle of aspects of ordinary life as people hide from the war outside their walls, disguising themselves.

> Outside there was marching
> ...A warmth
> started to radiate within me...
> it was if another body had been
> hooked into my blood circulation.

The poet notes that survival and recovery live with each other in the intricate way that survival is both a way to remind ourselves that life continues as well as the temporary purchase of a necessary denial of what is happening to us.

Trauma generally displaces us from safe and familiar circumstance, but exile is the most literal displacement. When it hits us, we are jettisoned into an unknown space or a space we hate for what it means to us. This space can be physical, or it can be emotional. In writing about exile, poets speak mostly of the physical displacement, the actual move away from home which, of course, is emotional in its terror. Nazand Begikhani writes about the aftermath of the chemical bombing of Halabja by Saddam Hussein's forces in 1988, which took 5,000 lives, mostly women and children. Begikhani writes,

> I buried that false self
> and cried for the real one
> that once was me...
> which no longer belongs to me
> but always breathes inside me.

The poet speaks to the central issue of recovery in ways that play the chord of the meaning of the word, to recover, to find and reclaim that which has been lost or pushed away to some difficult place inside us.

Poetry itself is enlivened by generosity, and this collection is a solid act of generosity. It is this gift of testimony from poets across a broad range of experience and language, poems that tell us we can gather ourselves from the shock of upset and loss in life and continue. We can move onward. We can work to reclaim that real self that breathes inside us.

It seems appropriate to close as I began, by revisiting Dr. King's death, for it shows us the connectedness of our lives. His death was a national trauma, and life-shattering events that are national do touch all the various personal challenges we face in life. Those who were caring for terminally ill loved ones looked up from their nursing stations, perhaps to shed a tear or to grimace when they heard the news. Those making preparations to bury a lost child were perhaps further grieved. Those soldiers on combat duty in Vietnam and those caught elsewhere in wars perhaps felt life's precarious nature more deeply if they heard the news. Giving credence to John Donne, even those adverse to his project in life have to live with the subtle way his contribution touches their lives. The bell tolls for each of us, and these poems show us the resonance of this ringing as we go about from day to day. The bell tolls for goodness and wholeness in our lives, and this is what this anthology seeks to do for the reader as it draws from the lives of people who have struggled with trauma and tragedy.

After Shocks: The Poetry of Recovery for Life-Shattering Events is a book that seeks to stand up and walk among us as a living thing, a force to activate the good and prepare us to weather the bad.

Let it stand and not be taken down. Let it live in our lives as readers.

Afaa Michael Weaver
Alumnae Professor English
Simmons College
Boston, Massachusetts

The Distance Between the Way We Die and the Way We Live

by Nicholas Mazza

I have started and stopped writing this foreword many times, perhaps because it would mean having to re-experience the traumatic loss of my own 21 year-old son Chris, killed in a car crash on Nov. 1, 2005. It would also mean I would be saying good-bye again. Not that a day goes by that I don't think of Chris or try to do something in remembrance of him, but I know about the power of words.

Poetry compels us to feel deeply, think without restrictions, and stand on sometimes-shaky ground. I have been engaged in the study, practice, and teaching of crisis intervention (with significant attention to death and other forms of loss) and poetry therapy for over 30 years. My expertise in the area of death and loss seemed more of a cruel joke than an aid in trying to deal with the unimaginable. Of course, in my graduate social work classes, I inform my students that all clinical models of grief are imperfect and serve only as a guide. Life is generally not that predictable and orderly. Death and loss can show up as uninvited guests at the strangest times. And the relationship between life and loss is not always linear. "Closure" is an often misused and inadequate term. Life is indeed a series of losses, and opportunities. The often reductionist approaches to death and loss in the social and medical science literature lend toward a mechanical approach to education and clinical practice. Increasingly the call in the professional literature of the helping professions is evidenced-based practice usually referring to quantitative research. This is fine but not sufficient. Poetry is research of the highest order. It is only through language, symbol, and story that we truly understand individuals, families, and communities. It is only through language (verbal and nonverbal) that we make meaning, form relationships, and promote healing/growth. Finally, I realized that through poetry we could say good-bye and sustain life in the same motion.

Tom Lombardo, the editor and contributing poet, drawing from his own artistic abilities and personal experience has crafted a book of poetry from authors representing 15 nations that is compelling because it deals with both the pain and promise of life-shattering events. Death and loss cut across all countries. Perhaps the anguish that tears us apart also holds the greatest hope to bring us together. We are not alone. Turning tragic and life-altering experiences into poems is the distance between the way we die and the way we live. Loss is both unique to each person and universal to humankind. Each poem in this collection is evidence that poetry transcends time and space.

Recovery doesn't mean "finished." In this collection of poetry, recovery is not meant to imply the outcome of bereavement but rather speaks to transformation and hope. Recovery in effect is very personal and subjective that relates to the individual's belief system, culture, developmental stage, and role. Recovery involves the seemingly contradictory process of both letting go and living with the loss. This process, however, can bring new meaning and purpose to one's life. Many of the poems can help individuals acknowledge the reality of their losses and develop an understanding that helps them continue on their life journey. There are no short cuts in dealing with death and loss. It cannot be medicated or denied indefinitely without some problematic consequence. The permanency of loss can be shaped into a new story. This international collection of poetry can serve as an aid in promoting compassion and courage. We draw courage from those on a similar path. Our stories, whether personal or professional, are about transitions, and the story continues to unfold.

Consider the range and depth of loss that is conveyed from lines in some of the selected poems organized around types of losses—death of spouse, war, exile, abuse, addiction, bigotry, loss of child, divorce/loss of lover, innocence, illness/injury, and death of family members/friends:

Recovery from the death of a spouse

In reading Donald Hall's "Letter After a Year," which was written to his dead wife, poet Jane Kenyon. I found myself both laughing and crying at the same time when I came to the lines about him visiting the graveyard with his dog Gus:

> Every day Gus and I
> take a walk in the graveyard.
> I'm the one who doesn't
> piss on your stone.

Tom Lombardo's poem "Daffodils" captures the practical aspects of going on with life, the technical demands, family relationships, and a glimpse of life through nature:

> For weeks after Lana's funeral,
> my mother cooked for me,
> handled death's paperwork,
> opened a door——
> Looking outward for the first time since burial
> prayers, I saw daffodils blooming.

Recovery from war

War veteran Doug Anderson's "Outliving Our Ghosts" speaks to surviving the Vietnam War:

> Talking again we honor the darkness
> breathe again the sweet air of a second life.
> We are here and we are whole.
> I hold the X-ray up to the light:
> the fragments still in your flesh,
> bright winter scars.

Recovery from exile

Lines from the poem "To the Children of Prison and Exile" by Majid Naficy, whose wife was executed by the Iranian government, perhaps capture the essence of this collection:

> After the silence of firing squads...
> I want to turn this death into life...
> I want to turn this death into beauty...
> I want to turn this death into a poem...
> I want to turn this death into life.

Recovery from abuse

Barbara Mitchell's "Small Courage" offers larger hopes:

> Twelve years of love smashed into my eyes
> to realize
> true gifts are not intrusive
> they do not bind the spirit…
> I reinvent myself on new hope.

Recovery from addiction

Clinton Campbell's "Club Soda Nights" speaks to the long journey toward recovery from alcoholism:

> She takes my hand, asks if I'm OK,
> and we take the long way home.

Recovery from bigotry

Having spent three years in a Stalinist prison camp, György Faludy's *Farewell to Recsk* (translated from the Hungarian by Paul Sohar) speaks to the power of poetry:

> Now I am ashamed to say it was easier for me, all my pains
> and troubles were numbed when I wove them into poetry.

Recovery from the loss of child

"Michelle" by Gail Rudd Entrekin hit closest to home for me. The poem speaks to silent pain and the importance of purpose and support:

> Leaving the restaurant, someone
> holds the door for her. People fall back
> and away, avoiding her circle of despair.

But two women who know she has lost a child,
walk close, their hands gently touching
her back, taking her arms, leaning their
warm bodies into hers.

Recovery from divorce or loss of lover

"Criss Cross Apple Sauce" by Thomas Lux addresses the far reaching impact of divorce on families:

My daughter sings,
my daughter with her buffalo-size heart,
my daughter brilliant and kind,
my daughter singing
as we drive from her mother's house to mine.

Recovery from loss of innocence

"We Lose Our Innocence" by Kurtis Lamkin captures the developmental aspects of loss:

We lose our innocence believing.
Arrival begins the great festival of loss.
Just when we realize the mystery is the beauty
it's time to go.

Recovery from illness or injury

A few months after kidney transplant surgery, J.E. Pitts assesses his body in "Scar Inventory," and keeps us wondering:

All the scars will heal one day—
at least that's what the doctors say.

Recovery from the death of family or friends

In "The Immense," Joseph Enzweiler mourns the death of his father but also addresses the developmental aspects of loss:

> Look hard one time
> at the man he had been.
> When I turn and let him go,
> I am a little boy again.

I learned from Ted Bowman, my good friend and colleague at the National Association for Poetry Therapy, that perhaps the most significant loss is the loss of the dream, the loss of how we imagined our lives would be in the future—the loss of a limb curtailing a promising athlete's future, a divorce ending the dream of how an individual imagined his or life would be with the other through the years, the death of a child ending the dream of a parent's wish for how his/her son or daughter would grow and find happiness.

This collection of poetry is both voice and inspiration for all those who dare to recognize loss as a part of life, pain as a part of joy, and language as a part of hope. Although there will always be an empty space on anything that I write, I remind myself that reflection can become remembrance and this becomes a legacy for those who have gone before us. It is through poetry and story that we create meaning and form relationships.

May your poem and story always remain unfinished.

Nicholas Mazza, Ph.D.
Editor, *Journal of Poetry Therapy*
Patricia V. Vance Professor of Social Work
Florida State University College of Social Work
Tallahassee, Florida

Healing Comes Through Bold Voices
by Walter Brueggemann

Loss is an inescapable dimension of the human condition. But until we lose—or have lost—we tend not to notice. Once we have lost, the ache yearns for speech. The speech that is required by aching loss is not explanation. It is imagining in bold ways so that the loss can be seen and heard, served and honored by others.

In this remarkable volume, Tom Lombardo has rendered a peculiar service to us all. He has gathered the aching words of loss from many zones of the human condition by a panoply of poets. The sum of these poems is to tell the truth and by the telling to find relief and sometimes healing. The ones who read and hear these poems can share the loss that is so common among us, and perhaps also share the healing that comes through bold voice.

Walter Brueggemann, Ph.D.
William Marcellus McPheeters Professor of Old Testament (emeritus)
Columbia Theological Seminary
Decatur, Georgia

An Introduction to *After Shocks: The Poetry of Recovery for Life-Shattering Events*

by Tom Lombardo

On the afternoon of Saturday, April 13, 1985, my wife, Lana, was killed in an auto accident. I received a call at my office to come to the hospital immediately. She had been killed on impact. The policeman who had been at the scene was kind enough to come to the hospital to tell me, "She did not need the ambulance's siren." I bid goodbye to her lifeless body, with massive head injury, lying on a steel gurney. I found myself a widower in my early 30s, without peer among anyone I knew. Well-wishers offered condolences like this: "You're young. You'll get over this." Or "You're too young, you'll never get over this." I have spent the past two-plus decades coming to some understanding of my wife's death, my grief, and what recovery means in the context of my own life.

I've focused deeply within myself, and I've traveled far outside myself to reach out to others. I can remember the precise moment when the shock of what had happened fell way, and my recovery began. It was an extraordinary physical reaction as well as a deeply emotional sensation. I went from the pit of grief to goose-pimply elation, then, an hour later, back down into Hell again. But I somehow knew deep in my soul that I had begun to look forward.

During the decade after Lana's death, the wives of five of my friends died young: one from breast cancer and one from skin cancer, which are "normal" types of death, but the others: a scuba-diving accident, an asthma attack (while on honeymoon in Katmandu, Nepal), and a brain aneurysm. I spent time with those men, listening, sharing coffee, whisky, and what little consolation I could give, still trying to understand my own ongoing grieving in the context of their fresh devastation.

I have since started a new marriage and we have two lovely children. I still think about Lana and experience grief in some form every day, more intensely as the anniversary of her death approaches each year. I maintain contact with Lana's mother and sister. Her father, whom I was very close to, died a few years after she died, and I'm sure her death summoned his.

I'm not an expert nor a therapist. Just a guy who lived it. I look at my life now, and some days, I wonder: Have I recovered? Or is losing a spouse like living with alcoholism? What does recovery mean? What recovery I've experienced—how has that happened?

Reading poetry gave me solace during the early stages of my grief. I returned to some old favorites—Emily Dickinson, T.S. Eliot, e.e. cummings, Robert Frost—not a particularly soothing group, you might say, but for me, they were familiar from a time in my life when my life seemed more settled. The language, the music, the ghosts in the haunted house offered an escape from a life seemingly shattered—an escape from "if…then" "what if" "how" "why" questions plaguing my nights, questions that had no answers.

1985 was also the year of publication of Douglas Dunn's *Elegies* (Faber & Faber), which won the Whitbread Book of the Year. A dear friend gave me a copy, brought back from England. Though the circumstances of Leslie Balfour Dunn's death were quite different, I felt Dunn's world embrace me.

> Grief wrongs us so. I stand, and wait, and cry
> For the absurd forgiveness, not knowing why.

A few years later, Donald Hall's book *Without*, poems covering the illness and death of his wife, the poet Jane Kenyon, touched me in the same way.

These two books moved me deeply as books of recovery. They seemed direct, straightforward, and honest in their stories, emotion, and language.

It took several years for me to start writing about Lana's death and the aftermath—my continuing life. My first poems dismantled whatever blocks I had constructed, and from that point, I visited my grief and wrote. I wish I could say that writing provided immediate relief or a sense of peace or closure, but mostly the poems were painfully draining and during the months that I wrote the first burst of them, I became depressed and irritable. I felt at times that I was picking at a scab covering an infection—the wound had not healed, the scar was raw and needed to open and bleed into the sun's light. Over the long-term, writing the poems helped me find a healthier level of comprehension and acceptance.

Shock through acceptance—there is great disagreement among therapists as to the "stages of grief." Are there five? Three? Seven? Do they come in some order? Maybe it's a continuum, not discrete steps? But one thing seems clear to me. There is a process that begins with an event and proceeds to some form of acceptance, if not recovery. Sometimes it's the death of a spouse. But the event might also be an act of war. It might be deciding to leave, or being forced to leave, your homeland. It might be the bottom of the pit called addiction. It might be divorce. It might be the victimization caused by abuse or bigotry. It might be a serious injury or illness requiring life-threatening medical treatment. Events of life-shattering proportions require us to achieve some level of recovery.

Many contemporary poets are writing about these topics. Mary Jo Bang's *Elegy* relives her grief over the death of her son. Linda McCarriston wrote *Eva-Mary*, a heart-rending collection about growing up abused, which won the National Book Award. Sharon Olds wrote collections about childhood abuse and alcoholism. Others: Carolyn Forche, Bruce Weigl, Tess Gallagher, Marie Howe. Each poet has focused upon a topic of his or her own experience. Of the poets just mentioned, Bang is the one included here, but they all represent a chorus of voices in a growing sub-genre of recovery poetry.

What this anthology intends to do is show that the poetry of recovery cuts across many boundaries. What this anthology intends to accomplish is to provide its readers with a source of comfort in the language of poets who've experienced these events and have come to some kind of acceptance.

Some of the poets included in this anthology are well known award winners and Poets Laureate. Dunn and Hall are included here, writing about the deaths of their wives; Thomas Lux with a take on the daily routines of divorce; William Stafford on the death of his son Bret; Rita Dove on her foray into ballroom dancing as an act of recovery. But there is also the novelist Molly Gloss, in her first published poems, writing about the death of her husband, and Major Jackson meditating upon the passing of a friend and mentor, and Brian Turner's stunning poems from the Iraq war show even in their horror the seeds of his recovery, while Pam Bernard and Stellasue Lee write about their fathers and how they dealt long-term with their experiences in the world wars. Liu Hongbin, exiled from China for his protests at Tiananmen Square, writes of his discoveries, external and internal, along his way to London, where he now writes and publishes in English. Susan Meyers tells the story of the year she banished yellow as her mother's health declined. Ron Rash shows how people forced off their homeland by the Army Corps of Engineers can achieve a sense of closure with their past, which will soon be drowned by waters behind a dam. Laurel Blossom writes about the torment of the first 90-days of sobriety in a lengthy prose poem from her new book, *Degrees of Latitude*. The section of this anthology on bigotry brings together poems from African American poets Kevin Young and Randall Horton, the Indian poet Satyendra Srivastava, Nigerian poet Tolu Ogunlesi, Israeli poet Meir Wieseltier, and Hispanic American poet Richard Garcia. The loss of a child may be the most heart-rending horror possible in anyone's life, but indeed, even from this, there may be lessons in recovery as told by Iranian poet Farideh Hassanzadeh and Israeli poet Rachel Tzvia Back.

As in all aspects of real life, recovery may take unexpected turns into areas that lift the spirits with humor or irony, and in this anthology, lighter moments pop into view here and there: Satyendra Srivastava's twist on empire and exile in "Sir Winston Churchill Knew My Mother," Joy Helsing's shockingly funny take on her final defeat of a battering husband, the Roman Catholic poet Sister Lou Ella Hickman's surprising view of the maternal consequences of her vow of chastity, Rebecca McClanahan's wry imaginings of the "what-ifs" of infidelity, Carol Ann Duffy's unveiling of the interrupted grief of Mrs. Lazarus, Simon Armitage's litany for a Herculean collapse.

These few examples and all the poems in *After Shocks: The Poetry of Recovery for Life-Shattering Events* bear messages of recovery to its readers. The messages range from the raw beginnings to long-term acceptance. That couplet I quoted above from Dunn's sonnet "Kaleidoscope" served as a model for my editing. I searched for poems in all categories that contained a message of recovery through the language of poetry: Grief, War, Exile, Abuse, Divorce, Addiction, Injury, Illness, Bigotry, Loss of Innocence. I have tried to select poems for their clarity of story, emotion, voice, music, and language. I hope first that readers enjoy the reading, then I hope that the poems offer comfort, guidance, companionship, and healing.

Tom Lombardo
Editor
After Shocks: The Poetry of Recovery for Life-Shattering Events

Recovery From Death of a Spouse

Grief wrongs us so. I stand, and wait, and cry
For the absurd forgiveness, not knowing why

—Douglas Dunn

Carol Dine

Owl's Head

On the first night after you die, we make love.
Your tongue, a sparrow in my mouth.

On the second night, you dye
the white egg of a parrot in beet juice,
scratch snowflakes into the waxy shell.

On the third night, I boil a crow's blue egg
in vinegar; before it cools, I swallow it whole.

On the fourth night in Owl's Head,
we lie on the shore; the tide ambles in,
wrapping us in seaweed.
We swim away
together in our green green skin.

Douglas Dunn

The Kaleidoscope

To climb these stairs again, bearing a tray,
Might be to find you pillowed with your books,
Your inventories listing gowns and frocks
As if preparing for a holiday.
Or, turning from the landing, I might find
My presence watched through your kaleidoscope,
A symmetry of husbands, each redesigned
In lovely forms of foresight, prayer and hope.
I climb these stairs a dozen times a day
And, by that open door, wait, looking in
At where you died. My hands become a tray
Offering me, my flesh, my soul, my skin.
Grief wrongs us so. I stand, and wait, and cry
For the absurd forgiveness, not knowing why.

Cathy Smith Bowers

Whistle-Speak

Three weeks after your death
I found them, dog-eared,
flagged and marked, colorful
brochures you hoped

to tempt me with, a trip
you'd planned for years
to that tiny drift of islands
courting Africa's golden

cheek. Remnants of old
volcanoes, fallen ash
and chard, each island
a realm of gorges and ravines

radiating from their centers
like spokes of a wheel. Who
wouldn't want to go there,
where the second native language

is that of birds, shepherds whistling
their messages to an ear cocked miles
away. Where even insults mimic
the mating songs of doves. See

how this old denizen folds his little
finger, presses tight against his tongue
and blows, free hand a makeshift
megaphone cupping conjured sound,

a trill, a chirp, a squawk
surfing the crags and slopes
of no man's land. *It can be used*
for anything, the caption reads:

Call to your friend.
Gather home your children.
Find, in a crowd, the husband
you've somehow lost.

Tom Lombardo

Daffodils

For weeks after Lana's funeral,
my mother cooked for me,
handled death's paperwork,
opened a door—
Look outside at your back yard.
Looking outward for the first time since burial
prayers, I saw daffodils blooming,
the ones that Lana and I had planted
in a sunken rectangular spot last Fall,
set against the bright, new green of Spring,
Easter white and careless yellow.

Patricia Wellingham-Jones

Your Shoes

Barbara the Hospice nurse
tossed your shoes
under my office chair
when we carried your body
wrapped in your sheets
out to the gurney.
I feel comforted
every time I look
at those shabby shoes
worn down at the heel
with Velcro straps frayed
and fuzzed with lint.
I picture your little
white-sock-clad feet
poking into the shoes
with my help.
I'm leaving them there
as long as that comfort lingers.

Simon Armitage

Poem

Frank O'Hara was open on the desk
but I went straight for the directory.
Nick was out, Joey was engaged, Jim was
just making coffee and why didn't I

come over. I had Astrud Gilberto
singing 'Bim Bom' on my Sony Walkman
and the sun was drying the damp slates on
the rooftops. I walked in without ringing

and he still wasn't dressed or shaved when we
topped up the coffee with his old man's Scotch
(it was only half ten but what the hell)
and took the newspapers into the porch.

Talking Heads were on the radio. I
was just about to mention the football
when he said 'Look, will you help me clear her
wardrobe out?' I said 'Sure Jim, anything.'

Donald Hall

Independence Day Letter

Five A.M., the Fourth of July.
I walk by Eagle Pond with the dog,
wearing my leather coat
against the clear early chill,
looking at water lilies that clutch
cool yellow fists together,
as I undertake another day
twelve weeks after the Tuesday
we learned that you would die.

This afternoon I'll pay bills
and write a friend about her book
and watch Red Sox baseball.
I'll walk Gussie again.
I'll microwave some Stouffer's.
A woman will drive from Bristol
to examine your mother's Ford
parked beside your Saab
in the dead women's used car lot.

Tonight the Andover fireworks
will have to go on without me
as I go to bed early, reading
The Man Without Qualities
with insufficient attention
because I keep watching you die.
Tomorrow I will wake at five
to the tenth Wednesday
after the Wednesday we buried you.

Donald Hall

Midwinter Letter

I wanted this assaulting winter
to end before January ended.
But I want everything to end.
I lean forward from emptiness
eager for more emptiness:
the next thing! the next thing!

The thaw arrived as the front loader
departed: warm sun, slush, then
forty-eight hours of downpour.
Snowdrifts decomposed by the house.
Walker Brook tore ice blocks
loose with a clamor
that worried Gus as we walked
beside the filthy flesh
of old snow.

    I parked
on Route 4 by the graveyard,
wearing my new Christmas boots
that your brother's family gave me,
and hiked to your grave.
The snow was a foot deep, but stiff,
and I sank down only a little.
Gus danced and skittered, happy,
but not so happy as I was.

One day the temperature dropped
to zero, so icy I couldn't
walk Gus, and my knees hurt
like my mother's. Following
your advice, I took Advil.
I forgot to tell you: My tests
are good, no cancer, and my sugar
is stable. Sometimes for a week
I have trouble sleeping,
especially after a nightmare
when you leave me for someone else.

One weekend Andrew's family
stayed over for the night.
All three of the children
sat on my lap while I read stories
—and Emily liked my meatloaf.
Sometimes I read these letters aloud
to our friends.

                When you wrote
about lovemaking or cancer,
about absences or a quarrel,
I loved to turn up in your poems.
I imagined those you'd make
after I died; I regretted
I wouldn't be able to read them.

Although it's still light
at 5 P.M., the feeder goes unattended.
The woodpecker has done
with my suet for the day.
Red squirrels doze in their holes.
Chickadees sleep in the barn
or up hill in hemlock branches.

I want to sleep like the birds,
then wake to write you again
without hope that you read me.
If a car pulls into the drive
I want to hide in our bedroom
the way you hid sometimes
when people came calling.

Remembered happiness is agony;
so is remembered agony.
I live in a present compelled
by anniversaries and objects:
your pincushion; your white slipper;
your hooded Selectric II;
the label *basil* in a familiar hand;
a stain on flowery sheets.

Donald Hall

Letter After a Year

Here's a story I never told you.
Living in a rented house
on South University in Ann Arbor
long before we met, I found
bundled letters in the attic room
where I took myself to work.
A young woman tenant of the attic
wrote these letters to her lover,
who had died in a plane crash.
In my thirtieth year, with tenure
and a new book coming out,
I read the letters in puzzlement.
"She's writing to somebody *dead*?"

There's one good thing
about April. Every day Gus and I
take a walk in the graveyard.
I'm the one who doesn't
piss on your stone. All winter
when ice and snow kept me away
I worried that you missed me.
"Perkins! Where the hell
are you?"

       In hell. Every day
I play in repertory the same
script without you, without love,
without audience except for Gus,

who waits attentive
for cues: a walk, a biscuit,
bedtime. The year of days
without you and your body swept by
as quick as an afternoon;
but each afternoon took a year.

At first in my outrage
I daydreamed burning the house:
kerosene in pie plates
with a candle lit in the middle.
I locked myself in your study
with Gus, Ada, and the rifle
my father gave me at twelve.
I killed our cat and our dog.
I swallowed a bottle of pills,
knowing that if I woke on fire
I had the gun.

          After you died
I stopped rereading history.
I took up Cormac McCarthy
for the rage and murder.
Now I return to Gibbon; secure
in his reasonable civilization,
he exercises detachment
as barbarians skewer Romans.
Then Huns gallop from the sunrise
wearing skulls.

          What's new?
I see more people now. In March,
I took Kate and Mary to Piero's.

At the end of the month ice dropped
to the pond's bottom, and water
flashed and flowed
through pines in western light.
The year melted into April
and I lived through the hour
we learned last year you would die.
For the next ten days, my mind
sat by our bed again
as you diminished cell by cell.

Last week the goldfinches
flew back for a second spring.
Again I witnessed snowdrops
worry from dead leaves
into air. Now your hillside
daffodils edge up, and today
it's a year since we set you down
at the border of the graveyard
on a breezy April day. We stood
in a circle around the coffin
and its hole, under pines
and birches, to lower you
into glacial sand.

        When I dream
sometimes your hair is long
and we make love as we used to.
One nap time I saw your face
at eighty: many lines, more flesh,
the good bones distinct.

It's astonishing to be old.
When I stand after sitting,
I'm shocked at how I must stretch
to ease the stiffness out.
When we first spoke of marriage
we dismissed the notion
because you'd be a widow
twenty-five years, or maybe
I wouldn't be able to make love
while desire still flared in you.
Sometimes now I feel crazy
with desire again
as if I were forty, drinking,
and just divorced.

Ruth Houghton had a stroke.
Her daughter sent me the album
of photographs Roger took
in his documentary passion—
inside and outside our house,
every room, every corner—
one day in September 1984.
I howled as I gazed at that day
intact. Our furniture
looked out of place, as if vandals
had shoved everything awry.
There were pictures on the walls
we put away long ago.
The kitchen wallpaper shone
bright red in Roger's Kodacolor;
it faded over the years
as we watched, not seeing it fade.

Carol Ann Duffy

Mrs. Lazarus

I had grieved. I had wept for a night and a day
over my loss, ripped the cloth I was married in
from my breasts, howled, shrieked, clawed
at the burial stones till my hands bled, retched
his name over and over again, dead, dead.

Gone home. Gutted the place. Slept in a single cot,
widow, one empty glove, white femur
in the dust, half. Stuffed dark suits
into black bags, shuffled in a dead man's shoes,
noosed the double knot of a tie round my bare neck,

gaunt nun in the mirror, touching herself. I learnt
the Stations of Bereavement, the icon of my face
in each bleak frame; but all those months
he was going away from me, dwindling
to the shrunk size of a snapshot, going,

going. Till his name was no longer a certain spell
for his face. The last hair on his head
floated out from a book. His scent went from the house.
The will was read. See, he was vanishing
to the small zero held by the gold of my ring.

Then he was gone. Then he was legend, language;
my arm on the arm of the schoolteacher — the shock
of a man's strength under the sleeve of his coat —
along the hedgerows. But I was faithful
for as long as it took. Until he was memory.

So I could stand that evening in the field
in a shawl of fine air, healed, able
to watch the edge of the moon occur to the sky
and a hare thump from a hedge; then notice
the village men running towards me, shouting,

behind them the women and children, barking dogs,
and I knew. I knew by the sly light
on the blacksmith's face, the shrill eyes
of the barmaid, the sudden hands bearing me
into the hot tang of the crowd parting before me.

He lived. I saw the horror on his face.
I heard his mother's crazy song. I breathed
his stench; my bridegroom in his rotting shroud,
moist and disheveled from the grave's slack chew,
croaking his cuckold name, disinherited, out of his time.

Molly Gloss

Grief Moves out of the House

At first he tells you he's just stepping out to the porch
      for a quick cigarette
or down the block to pick up donuts, a newspaper.

Then one day he doesn't show up for lunch
or he takes off early in the morning
      before you've finished your coffee;
he doesn't come home for hours.

His things start to go missing—
      clothes, books—
he leaves you so slowly, piece by piece,
palming the little stuff, walking the big things
      out the door while you're distracted by the television
      or standing at the stove stirring risotto,
by the time you realize what's happening
      it's really too late to say anything:
your own shoes and sweaters have spread out
      across the closet and you're loath
      to give up the new space.

He stays out half the night, God knows where,
but sometimes you forget to lie awake
      listening for his key in the lock.

Then he's gone for days and weeks,
shows up on holidays, birthdays, anniversaries
      as if he's never been gone,
sits down with you just long enough
      for a stiff whiskey and a good cry.

Years later he still comes by,
pops in the door without calling first,
catches you in the shower or in bed—
after all this time no longer intimate
          you reach for something to cover your nakedness.

He hasn't entirely moved out, even now:
every so often you open a drawer or shift books on a shelf,
find some small thing he's left behind,
think: Maybe it's something he'd want you to hang onto.

You haven't changed your locks.
You haven't asked him for his key back.

Molly Gloss

Apocrypha

I find (after this long) it is not him
I miss but his witnessing

the mundane, momentous happenings
of my life as they stream by immaterial,

his bearing out that *this* happened,
and *this*, that he could be counted on

to remember that in February, yes,
the bled-white moon on clear nights

limned branch and branch of bare alder
across the wall above our bed.

I find (after this long) what I miss
is our lying together in darkness

beneath cast shadow, telling quietly
that *this* happened, then *this,*

affirming the whole and the shape
of our existence, each and together.

Tom Lombardo

Birthday Present

Window open to Namesti Square,
midnight air, breezes, trash flutters.
Flakes from coal-fired electricity
reflect the sparks of the Namesti trolley,
its hourly bells pealing me to sleep
in a two-room flat, my new wife next to me.

Sparks and ashes, my first wife, Lana,
awakens me, she leads me to light
and Formica. She hands me tablet and pen.
She whispers. I write down pieces of an afterlife.

Did you find your birthday present in the car?
Did it spill onto the hood?
You loved woolen ties in winter.
Did I splatter it with blood?
Have you worn it yet for her?

Before I answer, she's through the window,
I inhale what's left of the coal-flake air.
Namesti trolleys pealing me to sleep,
sparks, flashes, rising summer suns.
My wife, Hope, awakens
to ash on the windowsill.

Recovery From War

To sand go the skeletons of war, year by year

—Brian Turner

Thomas Lux

Letter to Walt Whitman from a Soldier He Nursed in Armory Square Hospital, Washington, D.C., 1866

dear Walt, kind uncle, its near two years since I left Armory Sq.
& I'm home now. The corn grew good this summer and we
bought 2 cows. My leg ain't right still but it's still my leg. When
you prommiced they wouldn't take it was the first time after the
grapeshot I didn't want to go to the world where there is no
parting. Dear Uncle, we have had a son borned & we call him
Walter Whitman Willis, he is well & Bright as a dollar. Yrs
Affectionately, Bill Willis

Pam Bernard

[As the landscape turns melancholic]

As the landscape turns melancholic,
mysterious, he knows he is near home: Asnabrüch.
Villages of whitewashed, half-timbered
houses capped with thatch, streams
banked with bog myrtle, old lime trees,
mottled, abundant. He's struggled
with his pack and rifle, so heavy
he's barely managed to keep them aloft.

At last, the familiar latch,
and at the top of the stairs, fragrance
of potato cakes, mother and young Hilda
busy with Saturday cooking. A jar of whortleberries
squats on the worn wooden table.

Later, under an aegis of his beloved
chestnut tree the sun glints with purpose
through the branches onto his clean hand—

yet he can think of nothing but returning
to the front, to what he understands—death
and stink, the mind-numbing boredom,
to the only life he now can live.

On sentry, he'd heard the unburied
dead belch and hiss, too far
in no-man's land to retrieve.
When the French sent up a star shell,
a headless corpse jerked as if startled
by the sudden illumination.

Elizabeth Bernardin

Catharine's Book

In my hands now so many years later
this frayed book owned by a woman
I never knew, her words on the frontispiece:
"Rather hard on a girl not to say
goodbye, don't you think?"

A lovers' spat: "I forgave you
and hunted for you at the station,"
she wrote, maybe brushing back a strand
of red hair slipped from its knot at the back
of her neck.

The pages in this book, Kipling
The Barrack-Room Ballads and Catharine
sincerely wishes him luck: "I'm almost glad
you missed my teary farewell," her eyes
looking away from the leather bound volume,
small, slim and red, its cover soft like doe skin.

She placed her pen nearby, closed
the cover, turned it over in her hands,
book edges smooth, and remembered
how she searched, he gone away,
the soldier off to war—Europe or some
warrior place—their ballad unsung,
train emptying out of the station.

Sándor Kányádi
      translated from Hungarian by *Paul Sohar*

Wartime (*Háború*)

We retreated into the cellar,
behind vats and mounds of carrots;
we had to squash and squeeze against each other:
farthest behind and almost underneath
the nubile girls disguised as old hags
with black kerchiefs and soot smeared on their cheeks.
Outside there was marching, wagons and guns and
tanks were rumbling: the front-line was
either retreating or advancing. A warmth
started to radiate within me,
the same kind I used to feel
on spring nights on the hard
boarding school bed:
outside the armies were beginning
to rumble to the beat of the
re-opened power plant;
it was as if another body had been
hooked into my blood circulation: a pair
of tightly squeezed thighs, a pair of
panting breasts were advancing closer and closer.
The girls were tittering, the wilted lads were
shushing. "The others are doing the same thing,
you silly ass," whispered a hand,
not under my clothes but my skin.
"A grown lad you are, lucky thing
for you I'm not on the draft board,"
said a young war widow laughing
as she straightened out her skirt
with an experienced hand when

the door was opened, giving an all
clear signal; and she followed behind
the soot-smudged girls as they marched out
in single file with eyes downcast
up the cellar steps.
Her two bent knees kept the cellar bright
with their beauty
for some time. And as to the war? I declared victory.

Stellasue Lee

Out of Nowhere

...this morning, me hiding in the closet
at seven. My father in the kitchen
of that small California Court apartment
past midnight. Across the center pathway
all the lights of the other houses dimmed to darkness
and him—with another freshly poured drink
talking to the dead men in his unit, those men
back who road the waves toward the shore
of Omaha Beach, those rolling waves,
the boat about to fall open, that trembling boat—
sweet mother of Jesus, into the cold water they went,
rifles above their heads, have mercy, pray
for us all in the hour of our need...

Doug Anderson

Outliving Our Ghosts
    —for Al Miller

You show me the X-ray,
tell me how the bullet clipped the rim of your helmet,
sheared off the top of your ear,
continued downward into the shoulder
where the nerves cable under the collarbone,
soft as the white of an eye, and there,
broke up and stopped. The Jews say,
Bad times past are good to tell of.
Al, did we dream it all?
With your fingers you trace bullet fragments,
how they have moved over the years
as your body continued its path toward the death
that touched your shoulder twenty years ago
and spun you back into life with your eyes open.
Flesh alive then is no longer part of us.
If each cell is new every seven years,
what is the heart's tattoo?
And the years between. You finding Buddha
in a young Vietnamese you killed;
me getting sober, seeing my life stand up
as from the tall grass,
where it had lain all this time, covered with signs.
Talking again we honor the darkness,
breathe again the sweet air of a second life.
We are here and we are whole.
I hold the X-ray up to the light:
the fragments still in your flesh,
bright winter stars.

Jim McGarrah

Peace

A small green fruit grows
only from the earth in Hue. Seeded
by the Cay Vai tree, it rises round
and moist in soil blood-red with memories.

I share it now with my friend
Vo Que at the Garden Café
just off a dirt trail in this city where
my heart stopped singing
so many years ago, silenced
in a battle to claim what was never mine.

Que and I are two poets grown old
by sharing one dream from different worlds.

Here, in this jungle heat beneath lavender
blossoms and banyan trees that once shaded
tanks, rifles, mines, and death,
we speak of hope. A voice within
us both chants in counterpoint harmony
beyond our separate tongues. Sometimes,
it makes the rustle of a spring rain,
the cry of geese in the gray dawn,
the whistle of wet wind through bamboo,
the drum of the Perfume River
beating ceaselessly on the stones of shore.
Sometimes, it whispers like a child's smile
or sunrise cracking a robin's egg sky.

I have traveled ten thousand miles,
decades through tormented time
and shattered space to hear
this voice rise within me once more
as I share a simple meal
with my friend, who, like the Cay Vai,
no longer bears me malice for crimes
I committed in my youth.

Jim McGarrah

March Is the Cruelest Month

Two robins and two jays trill
in counterpoint harmony as if Davis,
Coltrane, Parker, and Kirk flitted limb to limb
and spoke of various drugs and women
through the language of wind.

One leaf appears on a tree. You see it
through the bedroom window
and, like a caretaker in a cemetery,
sell yourself the illusion of rebirth
so you don't go crazy counting graves.

A woman is here and so are the stars,
full of cold fire lighting your mind
with memory and possibility.
The hooker on Tu Do Street
forty years ago with her silk *ao dai*

open to expose a thigh
the color of Tupelo honey reflected
these same stars from a different world.
You wonder briefly if that might be big
in some Jungian way, this woman lying so near

to your beating heart, a muscle you would
gladly tear from your chest and offer
as a mere token of what you feel,
like an emerald in a velvet box, this woman
reminding you of how the past never

escapes the present, instead of vice versa.
It's always the subtle things, sandalwood
incense, the hiss of the teakettle on the stove,
the flicker of shadows along the candle-lit walls,
that flash the rocket round through your mind.

Then the room on Tu Do becomes the rubble
of your life. The dust and the cordite take away
your breath and the woman who no longer is
bleeds into the one you lay beside and love.
Then, you bury your face in her hair,
smell lavender and fear.

Sonja Besford

subjects in the cold winter of '93/94 belgrade

it was the winter of looking for
coins down sofas and in wardrobes
to buy potatoes for the soup, milk
and bread perhaps, if lucky, while
pensioners scavenged rubbish containers
for potato-peel, soured milk at the
bottom of a tetra pack, stale bread;
it was the winter of releasing pet dogs
to see them join hungry packs and watch
their attacks on passers-by who carried
sticks and guns, shouted obscenities,
but at night, oh at night
in that defeated city of ditched joys
there was no sound except for the rabid
barking, round and round, on and on,
pointless like a prayer for an impossible
miracle, until a tired dawn broke
announcing old hungers and many new deaths
while undertakers sang heavenly songs

it was also the winter of merciless sanctions,
flying to budapest, bucharest, sofia or athens
boarding unheated buses onwards to belgrade
laden with medications, food and clothes
for family, friends and friends of friends
we drove through darkened villages
hamlets breathing with sinister silence
almost as venomous as mirrors in the house
of an aged actress who forgot all her lines

yet could see them all etched on her face;
we passed the lighted motel signs
neon invitations for ever cheaper joys
and stopped at a café in a petrol station
where unshaven unwashed men in bulging suits
sold smuggled petrol of dubious purity then rushed
to us mumbling offers to buy our foreign currency
and sell us anything we wanted, dead or alive;
we pretended not to be frightened, cool, cool
as if in a previous life we were all in al capone's
inner circle and were used to "pals" packing guns,
cool, cool about murdering and smuggling—
you can't harm me, we're such old mates, our
body language tried to signal as we trotted
across the tarmac in rhythm with the beat
of our terrified hearts;
unaware of the unstitched hem on her uniform
the waitress hobbled on her tired, flowering heels
to serve us tea with red hands which through
the years must have launched thousands of dirty
cups into soapy water,
exhaustion and illness stood still in her eyes
doubly locked by her unsmiling lips and we
hurried back to the sanctuary of our cold bus,
someone started to cry, someone else said,
may dear god help us all, and another voice
shouted, he left us long ago, and
still another above all others, fuck it all, let's sing!

Rachel Tzvia Back

(*what has anchored us*)

The ballast of their breathing
                    in the next room in the bed
beside in the darkened house
                    enchanted
                            breath expanding

to the rhythm of our fantasy:
                            buffalo stars
stampeding through
                    unblemished skies
above a sacred land we imagined
                            our own

The weight of the unwritten
                            truth
at well-bottom: rabid fear
            perched on the back of the absent
buffalo

The certainty of migrating cormorants
            in massive flocks their flight
                            path and patterns
absolute: they return every year
        to rest here

in the Huleh valley around the reflooded
    swamp of the north   where
I walk   October 2001
    one year after
        the women of Sakhnin first

buried their faces
        in the rough wind-dried still
            sweet smelling clothes of their
dead sons

Brian Turner

2000 lbs.

Ashur Square, Mosul

It begins simply with a fist, white-knuckled
and tight, glossy with sweat. With two eyes
in a rearview mirror watching for a convoy.
The radio a soundtrack that adrenaline has
pushed into silence, replacing it with a heartbeat,
his thumb trembling over the button.

A flight of gold, that's what Sefwan thinks
as he lights a Miami, draws in the smoke
and waits in his taxi at the traffic circle.
He thinks of summer 1974, lifting
pitchforks of grain high in the air,
the slow drift of it like the fall of Shatha's hair,
and although it was decades ago, he still loves her,
remembers her standing at the canebrake
where the buffalo cooled shoulder-deep in the water,
pleased with the orange cups of flowers he brought her,
and he regrets how so much can go wrong in a life,
how easily the years slip by, light as grain, bright
as the street's concussion of metal, shrapnel
traveling at the speed of sound to open him up
in blood and shock, a man whose last thoughts
are of love and wreckage, with no one there
to whisper him gone.

Sgt. Ledouix of the National Guard
speaks but cannot hear the words coming out,
and it's just as well his eardrums ruptured
because it lends the world a certain calm,

though the traffic circle is filled with people
running in panic, their legs a blur
like horses in a carousel, turning
and turning the way the tires spin
on the Humvee flipped to its side,
the gunner's hatch he was thrown from
a mystery to him now, a dark hole
in metal the color of sand, and if he could,
he would crawl back inside of it,
and though his fingertips scratch at the asphalt
he hasn't the strength to move:
shrapnel has torn into his ribcage
and he will bleed to death in minutes,
but he finds himself surrounded by a strange
beauty, the shine of light on the broken,
a woman's hand touching his face, tenderly
the way his wife might, amazed to find
a wedding ring on his crushed hand,
the bright gold sinking in flesh
going to bone.

Rasheed passes the bridal shop
on a bicycle, with Sefa beside him,
and just before the air ruckles and breaks
he glimpses the sidewalk reflections
in the storefront glass, men and women
walking and talking, or not, an instant
of clarity, just before each of them shatters
under the detonation's wave,
as if even the idea of them were being
destroyed, stripped of form,
the blast tearing into the manikins
who stood as though husband and wife
a moment before, who cannot touch
one another, who cannot kiss,

who now lie together in glass and debris,
holding one another in their half-armed embrace,
calling this love, if this is all there will ever be.

The civil affairs officer, Lt. Jackson, stares
at his missing hands, which make
no sense to him, no sense at all, to wave
these absurd stumps held in the air
where just a moment before he'd blown bubbles
out the Humvee window, his left hand holding the bottle,
his right hand dipping the plastic ring in soap,
filling the air behind them with floating spheres
like the oxygen trails of deep ocean divers,
something for the children, something beautiful,
translucent globes with their iridescent skins
drifting on vehicle exhaust and the breeze
that might lift one day over the Zagros mountains,
that kind of hope, small globes which may have
astonished someone on the sidewalk
seven minutes before Lt. Jackson blacks out
from blood loss and shock, with no one there to bandage
the wounds that would carry him home.

Nearby, an old woman cradles her grandson,
whispering, rocking him on her knees
as though singing him to sleep, her hands
wet with their blood, her black dress
soaked in it as her legs give out
and she buckles with him to the ground.
If you'd asked her forty years earlier
if she could see herself an old woman
begging by the roadside for money, here,
with a bomb exploding at the market
among all these people, she'd have said
To have your heart broken one last time

before dying, to kiss a child given sight
of a life he could never live? It's impossible,
this isn't the way we die.

And the man who triggered the button,
who may have invoked the Prophet's name,
or not—he is obliterated at the epicenter,
he is everywhere, he is of all things,
his touch is the air taken in, the blast
and the wave, the electricity of shock,
his is the sound the heart makes quick
in the panic's rush, the surge of blood
searching for light and color, that sound
the martyr cries filled with the word
his soul is made of, *Inshallah.*

Still hanging in the air over Ashur Square,
the telephone line snapped in two, crackling
a strange incantation the dead hear
as they wander confused amongst one another,
learning each other's names, trying to comfort
the living in their grief, to console
those who cannot accept such random pain,
speaking *habib* softly, one to another there
in the rubble and debris, *habib*
over and over, that it might not be forgotten.

Brian Turner

Night in Blue

At seven thousand feet and looking back, running lights
blacked out under the wings and America waiting,
a year of my life disappears at midnight,
the sky a deep viridian, the houselights below
small as match heads burned down to embers.

Has this year made me a better lover?
Will I understand something of hardship,
of loss, will a lover sense this
in my kiss or touch? What do I know
of redemption or sacrifice, what will I have
to say of the dead—that it was worth it,
that any of it made sense?
I have no words to speak of war.
I never dug the graves in Talafar.
I never held the mother crying in Ramadi.
I never lifted my friend's body
when they carried him home.

I have only the shadows under the leaves
to take with me, the quiet of the desert,
the low fog of Balad, orange groves
with ice forming on the rinds of fruit.
I have a woman crying in my ear
late at night when the stars go dim,
moonlight and sand as a resonance
of the dust of bones, and nothing more.

Brian Turner

To Sand

To sand go tracers and ball ammunition.
To sand the green smoke goes.
Each finned mortar, spinning in light.
Each star cluster, bursting above.
To sand go the skeletons of war, year by year.
To sand go the reticles of the brain,
the minarets and steeple bells, brackish
sludge from the open sewers, trashfires,
the silent cowbirds resting
on the shoulders of a yak. To sand
each head of cabbage unravels its leaves
the way dreams burn in the oilfires of night.

Martha Collins

After

After the scattering, after the nights of shattered
glass, broken stones, scrawls, marked
houses, chalked walls, after the counter
threats, shouts, shots against the scattered
unhoused stones, after the bombs from over
the ocean, the desert, after oil has mixed
with blood, after the blossoming desert is bombed
to sand and risen again to blossom, though this
is more than the story tells, the story, simply
begun with the scattering, ends with the gathering in
again from distant cities, countries, corners,
basements, caves where children were hidden, from graves
whose bones were moved to be burned, from ashes that would
not burn, from earth, from air, the people will come
together, they will ride in carts and trains
and cars, they will walk and run, and this
is the story, the people will cross the oceans,
they will cross the rivers on bridges made
of paper, blank and inked and printed and painted
paper bridges will bring them together, over
the waters the borders the wars will be over, under
the paper bridges that bridge the most the best we can.

Recovery From Exile

Exile will promise me
a turquoise land
and a wise tribe

—Nazand Begikhani

Nazand Begikhani

Illusion

I placed a yellow leaf
on the white wings of the wind
and let it go
then I heard a melody in the air:
"Exile will promise me
a turquoise land
and a wise tribe
where I am myself
and freedom is the friend of human beings"

Nazand Begikhani

The Wall

I woke up one day from a deep sleep
and found myself in a cold corner of the earth
brimming with uncertainty

I looked for the soft face of the sky
for the fresh smell of the sand after summer rain
and I looked for the lullaby of the trees
the serene silhouette of mother
and the subtle silence of father
I looked for the laughter of my baby sister
and for the peaceful presence of my brother

In a cold corner of the earth
brimming with uncertainty
I found myself faced with a naked wall
the silent stone of a refugee camp
reflecting the faded face of my father
the frozen laughter of my baby sister
A naked wall was standing still
reflecting the death of our brothers
who were unable to flee
the poisoning rain in Halabja
to take refuge here
in this cold corner of the earth

Nazand Begikhani

Exile

It was the end of a cold journey
The beginning of a silent season
I arrived in a sad island
where voices had a sharp music
and colour a different meaning
I began my first night
by shredding my forged passport
burying the dual person
that had consoled me on my solitary voyage
and talked for me at check points
I buried that false self
and cried for the real one
that once was me
the self that was left behind
on a fresh silvery hill
which no longer belongs to me
but always breathes inside me

It was the beginning of a blue season
the end of a long journey
I walked down the lonely lanes
in an unknown city
in search of a new voice
to chant for a wandering nation
I was in search of a magic mirror
that could reflect my whole being

Liu Hongbin

Spirit of the Sea

That song has been drowned.
Within the rushing waves, the surging, glancing light,
I have found my voice.

That life has been destroyed.
On a half-submerged rock, torn by the waves of the sea,
I have rediscovered my origins.

I want to build a new life.

Sea-gulls, nestling in light mist –
the wings of dreams in air –
time is a flock of gulls, taking wing and flying off
beyond the roar of the waves.

I am a demented wave thrown down on a reef,
instantly torn apart to reveal the explosion of light.
The pieces gather up to form
a contemplative surface, a rising and falling mirror for our gaze.

I am the petrel in the branches of sunlight.
I am the fish that melts in the sea.
I am the red-eyed lighthouse staring into the hurricane.
I am the suffering sail gathering the power of the wind.
I am the anchor that longs for the drifting wave.

Moonlight embellishes white marble
now running with glistening tears,
slowly slowly slowly fading.

The blind man tears the sun apart.

Through the colours of the night sea
I flee towards the edge of darkness,
climbing one blue ladder...

Liu Hongbin

The Unfamiliar Customs House

Nightmares waylaid me. I could hardly make a declaration to the customs officer. I had become a smuggler, dealing in nightmares. I was once again in exile.

When I took up my pen for the first time to write poetry I felt exiled from the ordinary world; then I was only a teenager. My exile was a voluntary one.

The night in London became damper. Sound flutters its wings hovering in the air. The lighted cigarette in my hand is like a sleepless eye.

The sky of the square in my mind seems to me still like a bloody, messy wound.

My frozen tongue has come alive. I want to speak.

The way I came is broken by the wind; the way back is muddy with anxiety. Paths beneath my feet run in all directions in the moonlight.

It is in that home where my childhood is stored. The mirror has forgotten its owner. Nobody there will turn on the table lamp to lift up the night. Books in the bookcase still have my fingerprints, which have gone cold between the pages. The hanging lamp no longer tenderly gazes down at the bed. The dust of time has covered all the nightmares and all the love. The windows which let in sunlight have gone blind. Is there any green mould secretly crawling over the uncarpeted floor?

In another place, Mother, through her glasses, fixes her eyes on the only photo of myself as a child, expecting my mischievous footsteps.

I want to go back, I must go back. The way swallowed by night has not yet come into sight. Night is like soft rocks blocking my way back. Let the rock of the night crash into me.

I want to go back. I want to go back home. But where is my home?

When I intrude into another country, an unfamiliar customs house appears before me. It is the yellow earth of my home, which receives me. I become buried, as it were, by the warm yellow colour? I can slumber soundly.

The nightmare has been detected and confiscated by the customs officer.

Paul Sohar

Redemption Circa 20th Century C.E.

A bucket and a scrubbing brush once cured me of
a panic attack that ferociously clung to my throat;

those modest tools were handed to me by a priest
in a crow-black cassock with a bony smile;

we were standing in the communal restroom,
the second focal point of the refugee camp,

the first being the window where
the bowls of soup were handed out,

but before you could work in the kitchen you
had to put in some time in the restrooms,

that was the rule in the refugee camp,
and as soon as I started working with

the bucket of water and the scrubbing brush
I heard angels explaining to me the scheme;

the smell of the latrine smelled sweet
after smelling fear for so long,

after smelling the cynical stench of hell
I was overcome by a smell of revelation,

the promise of salvation handed to me with
a bucket of water and a scrubbing brush.

Satyendra Srivastava

Sir Winston Churchill Knew My Mother

Sir Winston Churchill he knew India
He knew
Because India was to him the Kohinor
Of that Empire on which the sun never sets
Sir Winston also knew the town
Which his people had built for their comfort and ease
Cutting and carving it from the Himalaya's lap
– That child of the icy summits – that town
Which is called Mussoorie
Sir Winston knew where that town was and why
Because he had walked its long street rising and falling
Which had reminded him – somewhere somehow –
Of Princes Street in Edinburgh, another
Extremely beautiful town in the British Empire
And Sir Winston knew this too that
Also in the town called Mussoorie
A wave had risen
Shaking the foundations of Britain's Empire
The kind of wave that would seem to him
Just the folly of that crazy naked fakir of
India's national struggle
And Sir Winston knew this too that
In India some women who
Worshipped that same naked fakir as a father
Had laid down one day in the town of Mussoorie
In rows in the road and prevented the units
Of soldiers of the British Empire from going further
And among them had been some women who
Heavy with child could have given birth at any moment

Therefore exactly for this reason I
Went to Hyde Park Gate as soon as
I reached London
Stood in front of Sir Winston's shut house
Bowed respectfully, then spoke out loudly
'You, Sir Winston, knew my mother
Pregnant in her eighth month
Having received my father's blessing
She too laid down in
That road in Mussoorie
From where the army units had to return —
I am the son born from that mother's womb
And Satyendra is my name
And I have come to tell you
That I have now arrived in England.'

Marjory Wentworth

Linthong

1.
Waiting in the JFK IMMIGRATION LINE
Linthong drinks from a metal fountain.
Water circles in the back of his throat.

He opens his plastic bag for inspection:
one comb, a pair of Levis, and a knife.

2.
Swimming across
the Mekong River
open knife clenched
between his teeth
rope twisted
around the waist
of his sister
beside him
pulled under
ducking beneath
the moonlight
he dragged her
to a fishing boat
in the South China Sea

For weeks
they sailed with rice sacks
rigged to the mast
until a typhoon whipped
the cracked cotton to shreds

and pulled his sister
into the eager water.
When the winds died
they burned planks
torn from the deck,
boiled sea water to
catch steam in a tube
drops on the tongue

3.
In the Philippino camp,
ribs lined up
on his chest like a xylophone,
he learned English in the morning
and sold black market cigarettes
in the afternoon. Before he could sleep
he said the words milk and highway,
because he liked the sound.
He dreamed of California,
but he lives in Salem Massachusetts
in two rooms with eleven other people.
Every morning he goes to school
while the Lao fishermen take buses
to Gloucester to pack
fish into ice at the Gortons factory.

And the women stay behind
storing light bulbs, batteries,
and sneakers in the refrigerator,
leaving cooked rice and milk
in uncovered bowls on the cupboard.

4.
On Sundays Linthong chases sandpipers
in and out of the tide, pulsing
along the length of Singing Beach.

Dozens of spinnakers dot the horizon
like strange beautiful balloons.

He sits on a barnacled log,
tugs seaweed loose and chews.
Sucking on drops of ocean,
he watches fishermen
cast clear lines to the sea.

Diana Woodcock

Last Days of Summer

Shifting my tack, I'm on the James
kayaking—the prickle of faces,
events and names I thought I'd forgotten
a waterfall cascading down,
the daily manifestos and roll-call in the camp,
one line for resettlement, the other
repatriation, smell of whiskey on the border
guards' breath, children playing with shards
of shattered glass, hard-learned lessons of
what not to ask—what became of Sok Noth,
and who shot the woman pregnant with twins?

No one wanted to hear, so I locked these things
inside—got on with my life till I no longer cried.
And Somoen's cough, tubercular in the night,
ceased coming back to jolt me awake—I
somehow could have slipped her the medicine
that would have saved her, could have adopted
the one whose smile was the most timid—whose leg
had to be cut off above the knee. Still running to me
in my dreams, he still screams for help.

I breathe deep, smell of fish and promise of rain
in the air, sunset rays with a flair converging
like railroad tracks. Only days till leaves fall
and the James freezes over. Cormorants nap
on the decaying pier, ghosts skimming the river.
Overhead, a blue jay chases off a hawk twice its size.

Diana Woodcock

English as a Second Language

They come after a long day
spent working in the sun,
smiling unremittingly as if
they still believe they've done
the right thing. I teach them the
basics, they teach me about escape
and new identities.

Weary of their brave façades,
I've asked them to share something
from their countries that defines them.
Antonio from El Salvador offers us
shards of shrapnel taken from his side
the day he nearly died. Jose from Argentina
holds up a photograph of his father missing
for decades, and a memory that never fades.
As he slips back into Spanish, I remind him
gently, *Speak only English here.*
Khema from Cambodia brought a wooden
spoon and her mother holding it over the fire
the day Pol Pot's men came at noon to rape
and kill her while the children sat hidden
behind the rolled-up sleeping mats.

After they've each had a turn, I say,
*Tonight let's look at adjectives and practice
describing your dead and missing relatives.*
The lesson goes quite well—combination ESL
and grief workshop.

When the class is over, I watch them
gather up all they've brought. Each one
has reverted to the first language. I watch
them walking to their cars. Their feet
are made of glass.

Majid Naficy

To the Children of Prison and Exile

After the silence of firing squads
Still it burns in our hearts
And we carry their corpses
On our broken backs.
I want to turn this death into life.

How many companions,
Who in these years of defeat and execution
Created life from an embryo?
I am talking about the children of prison and exile:
Cheshmeh, *Roza*, and *Sulmaz*.

I want to turn this death into beauty
That like a jug of water
Becomes filled with the freshness of *Cheshmeh*,
And like a red rose
Blooms from the lips of *Roza*,
And like the word *Sulmaz*
Becomes evergreen.
I will sift, grind, and soften this death,
Until the children of prison and exile
Mold it into play dough.
I am calling you,
O newborns of years of pain,
The crocodiles in your painting
Have no teeth,
Because the names of their friends
Never crossed their lips.

I want to turn this death into a poem,
That can be read like magic
When the corpse of a butterfly
Carried by ants
Makes you remember the dead ones.

I want to turn this death into life.

Majid Naficy

Ah, Los Angeles

Ah, Los Angeles!
I accept you as my city,
And after ten years
I am at peace with you.
Waiting without fear
I lean back against the bus post.
And I become lost
In the sounds of your midnight.

A man gets off Blue Bus 1
And crosses to this side
To take Brown Bus 4.
Perhaps he too is coming back
From his nights on campus.
On the way he has sobbed
Into a blank letter.
And from the seat behind
He has heard the voice of a woman
With a familiar accent.
On Brown Bus 4 it rains.
A woman is talking to her umbrella
And a man ceaselessly flushes a toilet.

I told Carlos yesterday,
"Your clanging cart
Wakes me up in the morning."
He collects cans
And wants to go back to Cuba.
From the Promenade

Comes the sound of my homeless man.
He sings blues
And plays guitar.
Where in the world can I hear
The black moaning of the saxophone
Alongside the Chinese chimes?
And see this warm olive skin
Through blue eyes?
The easy-moving doves
Rest on the empty benches.
They stare at the dinosaur
Who sprays stale water on our kids.
Marziyeh sings from a Persian market
I return, homesick
And I put my feet
On your back.
Ah, Los Angeles!
I feel your blood.
You taught me to get up
Look at my beautiful legs
And along with the marathon
Run on your broad shoulders.

Once I got tired of life
I coiled up under my blanket
And remained shut-off for two nights.
Then, my neighbor turned on NPR
And I heard of a Russian poet
Who in a death camp,
Could not write his poems
But his wife learned them by heart.

Will Âzad read my poetry?
On the days that I take him to school,
He sees the bus number from far off.

And calls me to get in line.
At night he stays under the shower
And lets the drops of water
Spray on his small body.
Sometimes we go to the beach.
He bikes and I skate.
He buys a Pepsi from a machine
And gives me one sip.

Yesterday we went to Romteen's house.
His father is a *Parsee* from India.
He wore *sadra* and *kusti*
While he was painting the house.
On that little stool
He looked like a Zoroastrian
Rowing from Hormoz to Sanjan.

Ah, Los Angeles!
Let me bend down and put my ear
To your warm skin.
Perhaps in you
I will find my own Sanjan.
No, it's not a ship touching
Against the rocky shore;
It's the rumbling Blue Bus 8.
I know.
I will get off at Idaho
And will pass the shopping carts
Left by the homeless
I will climb the stairs
And will open the door.
I will start the answering machine
And in the dark
I will wait like a fisherman.

Shelley Davidow

Hemispheres

before the dawn a Zulu warrior jogs
along an icy freeway holds his spear
up high runs till he's swallowed by a fog
and then I'm back in some sweet childhood year
my bike the winter veld a leaping dog
dissolve my mother cries oh dear oh dear
her voice is drowned by thunder and the rain
leaks through the roof and ruins the books again

the African dawn chorus fill my head
no that's the kettle whistling and I should
get up and wake the warm child in my bed
make tea and toast turn on TV watch Good
Day Oregon but for a while instead
of early TV smiles and morning food
I rinse out cups to drumming of spring rain
watch water swirl the wrong way down the drain

J. P. Dancing Bear

A Brief Informal History

For us, there was never a Harry Houdini
who escaped from the boxes or from behind
the Bureau of Land Management fences.
There was Jim Thorpe, who ran in circles

better than anyone else. He ran like a caged wolf.
That was something we all knew.

Great fists rose from the west, drifted over
the plains and pounded us with thunder
as though we had always been corn

waiting to be reduced to meal in the unfurling fields.
Out of the east the real fists came.

From within the snowstorm of lies, we heard
tales of our own resistance. But we heard

too, the names of our fathers embossed in chrome
on the fenders of cars, on the labels of alcohol,
in the lonely glow of neon above cafes. We heard
the death song coming from the sky, loud
and piercing the way a bird of iron might sound.

And all our ghosts. Those boys who went to war
and fought like there might be a freedom hidden
somewhere in blood. They came back to our open-
armed ghostfathers, their faces yellowed
and parched by the long poverty of their lives.

Our boys went back to being unneeded as a stone—
waiting in the desert, petroglyph for all that is lost.

Margaret Chula

Equilibrium

In Sacramento, I was a newspaper man, but now I stuff
newspapers into cracks around the door frame, between
the floorboards and into knotholes to keep sand, wind
and rattlesnakes out of our barracks.

Here at Topaz, the Jewel of the Desert, I have become a carpenter.
I use my hands to make life in the camp bearable for my family.
When we arrived, our shack held nothing but four army cots.
For mattresses, we were given bags to be filled with straw.

I salvaged lumber from the yard to build crude furniture –
a table, chairs, and a few shelves. Emi borrowed a broom and
swept out the dust, then sewed curtains by hand to hang in
the window. My son made a pull toy from the lids of tin cans.

Mama came with us. She was an *Issei* and a poet.
One day she wandered into the desert and never came back.
I fashioned a box with no nails to hold her ashes.
Emi made an *ikebana* from tumbleweeds.

Beneath the shadows of barbed wire, I have discovered
the beauty of tools. How a plane can subdue the harshness
of wood, its cold steel a comfort in my palm. How a level,
with its bubble that does not freeze in winter, can offer levity.

I have learned how to face a sandstorm with a strip of cardboard
plastered with glue, then to use this sandpaper to smooth out
the incongruities of our lives. I have been shown the miracle
of precision and balance – how a hammer can straighten out
the bent backs of nails and make them useful again.

Major Jackson

Urban Renewal

XIII.

The backyard garden wall is mossy green
and flakes a craggy mound of chips. Nearby
my grandfather kneels between a row of beans
and stabs his shears into earth. I squint an eye,—
a comma grows at his feet. The stucco's
an atlas, meshed-wire continents with leaders
who augured hate, hence ruins, which further sow
discontent. We are weeding, marking borders,
a million taproots stacked in shock. Forty years
from a three-story, he has watched the neighborhood,—
postwar marble steps, a scrubbed frontier
of Pontiacs lining the curb, fade to a hood.
Pasture of wind-driven litter swirls among greasy
bags of takeouts. Panicles of nightblasts
cap the air, a corner lot of broken TVs empties
and spills from a suitcase of hurt. Life amassed,
meaningless as a trampled box of Cornflakes.
When a beggar cupped for change outside
a check-cashing place then snatched his wallet,
he cleaned a .22 revolver & launched this plot. Tidal
layers of cement harden men born gentle as the root
crops tended south, the city its own bitter shrine.
We crouch by watering cans. He pulls a paradise of kale
and shakes root-dirt that snaps like a shadow lost in time.
Tomato vines coil by a plot of herbs. Far from the maddening
caravan of fistfights, jacked-rides, drunkards,
my pen takes aim from the thumbnail of his yard.

Lisha Adela Garcia

Breathing Forward in America

James is the Americanized name
of my D.C. cabbie, who fled soil-starved
Nigeria, to drive me to the Hyatt from the airport.
The militias that killed his wife and children missed
him as he had gone to Lagos for work.

The angels say we imprint our path
before we arrive as babies. I chose stones
slung across my back in guilt.

Candelaria who cleans my toilet at the hotel,
came from El Salvador. She is a doctor.
Better a half-life with little dignity in work
than the scripts of violence tattooed on her flesh.

Their nightmares live in screams
I don't hear. Survival
memories are headstones
dedicated to savagery.

Music is what remains of their attempts
to breathe forward in America. James' long
fingers tap the steering wheel to a tune
in a language I have never heard.

Candelaria sways with a Mijares ballad
as she vacuums. I want
to believe my hand is free
of any nails I might have hammered
into their flesh,
but I know this cannot be true.

Ron Rash

Last Service

Though cranes and bulldozers came,
yanked free marble and creek stones
like loose teeth, and then shovels
unearthed coffins and Christ's
stained glass face no longer paned
windows but like the steeple,
piano, bell, and hymnals
followed that rolling graveyard
over the quick-dying streams,
the soon obsolete bridges —
they still congregated there,
wading then crossing in boats
those last Sunday nights, their farms
already lost in the lake,
nothing but that brief island
left of their world as they lit
the church with candles and sang
from memory deep as water
old hymns of resurrection
before leaving that high ground
where the dead had once risen.

Recovery From Abuse

I re-invent myself on new hope

—Barbara Mitchell

Annie Finch

Three Generations of Secrets

Is the sound of my loud carrying life a knell
far across your small ocean? Do you share
the secret that the months keep hidden there?
Is my past-filled pregnancy a hungry shell?
I think I will turn metal, like a bell,
so you can clapper my voice out, to where
the silent memories will echo care
and speak again. We'll sound our double spell,
swinging; we'll swing back then, to forgive
my mother's curve around the angry past—
and then her mother's. They were smothered, bound
and quiet. But we'll speak, and you will live,
tolling and striking what we know at last,
until you ring aloud with newer sounds.

Barbara Mitchell

Small Courage

It has taken twelve years
to break the vow of silence you made me swear to
twelve years of love smashed into my eyes
to realize
true gifts are not intrusive
they do not bind the spirit
You hostaged my days
with cruel imitations of love burning my wrists
and my hope bound in livid cords
around my throat

Even now
as I attempt to negotiate freedom
a smile crouches at the corner of your mouth
and the loud noise of your anger is black confusion on my skin

Still
I do not flinch
at the upsweep of your arm
as it moves to pronounce your final gift

A small courage stammers into being
and strength unfolds from the cowering past
I break free from our worn vow
like a snapped rib
and from the cracked well of my lips
I protest these years of madness

It has taken twelve years to forgive the starving destiny
locked within these limbs
Twelve years for my wounds to return to themselves

Now
I re-invent myself on new hope
shaped to the curve of *my* bone
New reason to live
warm as my own blood

Now
I recite a new vow
that does not bleed
from the mouth

Roseann Lloyd

Too Much Give

In yard goods, there's a yardstick nailed down
on the cutting counter, scissors on a string.
Every Ben Franklin is the same, even here
in Two Harbors, a tourist town. The maple floors slant
and give as you walk around, scanning
bolts of material lined up, piled up, some askew.
Beautiful colors, neon cottons, watery silks, pastel
jerseys. Today I find black velvet, gorgeous
for a crazy quilt, feather stitched with
lavender and gold. Now I'm fingering some blue cotton stars—
I'll know from the feel if there's too much give
to be of use. I dig through the remnant bin, scraps
for baby things, 37 cents. It's automatic, this bargain
hunting, goes back to the days over a dozen years now,
when I walked to town three times a week
with the baby in the stroller,
my life predictable as a clock.

Morning walks, afternoon naps
5:00, the first glass of French Columbard.
In the spring, bouquets of lilies from the yard.
6:00, cooking dinner. Baby down,
time for quilts, and books, stacks of books.
Time to wonder if he'll come home, if he'll
want dinner, if he'll be pissed
because dinner wasn't what
he wanted, *because...* I never got beyond the
because when he started hitting, my fear
held down by the brandy under the sink.
Nothing was better than being a mother.

That's what I said then. I got up every morning
on time, happy to see my baby. The baby
didn't know anything was wrong. That's what I said then.
I ran on schedule, so different from my college
stance—I laughed when I read Ben Franklin's diary, how
he agonized over his daily schedule! Now I
was the one walking to the Ben Franklin
making a schedule work.

That was a long time ago, and here I am
in the Two Harbors Ben Franklin, making an
unscheduled stop. The kids are intently picking out
embroidery thread—purple, Kelly green, and red.
They're weaving bracelets while riding
in the car. In fact, that's why we stopped,
they ran out of red. I look across
the cottons, see a young woman
holding her baby on her left hip, holding up,
with her right arm, a swatch of cloth with huge red
and white sailboats—red is the best of color for
baby quilts—red is the first color they can see.
The mother is gazing off, imagining a new design.

Everything that happens is supposed to happen:
I'm here today to forgive that girl,
to forgive her for sewing instead of writing,
for staying home when she should've run,
for drinking when she should've
dialed 911. I'm here to forgive her
for making a life of
remnants, for living a life with too much
give. She looks so frail and lonely
over there, the chunky baby laughing on her hip.

Joy Helsing

Turnabout

Pound a pillow
my therapist says
pretend it's him

I pummel and punch
hitting back
till my arms grow tired

Try a silent yell
my therapist suggests
get it out

I scream without sound
till my throat burns

Imagine he's small
my therapist urges
the way you felt

I picture him shrunken
six inches high
a dictator doll
strutting on little feet
ranting in a tinny voice
shaking a tiny fist
till at last I laugh
and make him disappear

Nehassaiu deGannes

Last Surviving Hymn to Hathor

Who leads us, moon-drunk, into clover
and sweeps the starch rectangle of the blank half
of the bed? *You love him? You love him not?*
Lolling on the dark howl's tambourine.
Honey, can't find true love 'cuz yuh too afraid to die.
The train is in the cattle yard again,
clattering up and down the lonely tracks.

Gourd of lullabies and rich dark earth,
what makes us cough, plump the pillow, rise
to take a piss, catch the distance lowing in our ears—
Is that Ella all *glissando*?
What floods our hearts with thunder?
The train is in the cattle yard again, clattering
up and down the lonely tracks.

Look how her tail's a metronome. Her eyes are bells
of iron. Those daddy-long-leg lashes flint and there are sparks
of hammered iron flying 'bout the room. She's crying
Why, when a man gets too close with a bunch of cow-slip
orchids growing from his fist, you cock your head, go very still—
wonder what he plans on doing with his other fist?
You're hiding in the cattle yard again.

Pull a ream of paper from the white shelf of sleep
"blankness + me = possibility unchained;"
and drown the tinkling cowbells in the toilet's oceanic hiss.
But our conductor drop kicks her orchestra again.
She's lounging on your moon-white pillow.
Fool, love won't find you. Can't find you.
Her bassoon now quaking all the orchids in the room.

Why not lay your head down on her chamois lap?
She's scattering an entire confluence for you
of what is done and gone and lost for good
Life's a dung-hill and you plant your seeds in that
of what's to come is yours and can be yours to trust
Not in punishment but in sanctified pleasure. Cross over.
Cross over. The train is in the cattle yard again.

Peter Cooley

A Place Made of Starlight

This is the woman I know to be my sister.
Wizened, apple-sallow, she likes her room dark
inside the nursing home's glare. She barely sees me,
black shades drawn against the radiant autumn day,
purple, hectic yellow streaming from the trees.
I stand and stare. One of us has to speak.

How are you? FINE. Why did I try to speak
as if we could talk, a brother and a sister
perched on the same branch of the family tree?
We share our parents. But the forest, suddenly dark,
dwarfs me always, now I'm here, where I see me,
fifty years back, ten years younger, even today.

She is a raven, I some tiny winged thing, me
she shouts down, I-me longing to speak,
to tell my parents how she beats me every day,
dark wings claiming she will be my sister
no matter what I suffer in the darkening dark.
I scramble out farther on the family tree.

Where are my father, my mother on the tree?
I am growing smaller inside myself each day
while my body lengthens, climbing larger in the dark
toward a moment when I will finally speak
about the wounds inflicted, purpling, by my sister.
Who will believe someone small as me?

Sometimes I think the silence contains me
even today, knowing I leaped from the tree,

discovering I could fly away from my sister
to land in a clearing in the woods that day,
a place made of starlight I could finally speak.
Released by telling others, I can wear the violet dark

luminous around me now, standing in the dark,
staring at my sister who is staring back at me,
neither of us knowing how or what to speak.
Does she remember what happened on that tree?
I screamed, jumping, the branch snapped on the day
I showed my parents the bruises from my sister

and the secret toppled, falling with the tree.
And bruised truth came home to belong to me:
Never, never speak up against your sister.

Paul Allen

Lapses

God has called me to live and work,
three states removed from David Petty. (Praise Him.)
Ninth and 10th grades, band practice, some practiced
while our director locked himself in the supply room
to belt down his morning supply.
Behind the tympani, Petty played me with the mallets,
chant, *c'mon c'mon, man, c'mon, c'mon chicken shit,*
whatsa matter, hit me, hit me, whatsa matter....
But I didn't know what was the matter.
I couldn't *c'mon c'mon.* Even unsaved
I turned the other cheek.
Social Studies, I would dream through my conquistadors
of painting him blue, skewering him
on a lodge pole and offering him to the god of maize.

Extra credit: If an automobile weighing 2,000 pounds travels 60 miles per hour on a
straight road, assuming no friction, how high will it bounce when it runs over David
Petty's mother?

Made friends with the enemy. Slept over.
When his breathing became heavy,
lying beside him I'd hit him at the country club,
stick a fork in his throat,
throw him on the cart of the *petits fours,*
roll him out to the pool, bite off his lower lip,
tear a huge chunk of cheek out with my back teeth
while the membership looked on.
Part of the fantasy always went: The nurses
and orderlies were kind to me.

At home, (even late nights in my underwear)
I practiced for hours with my father's pistol
strapped to my hip, fast draw in the mirror at myself.

I've let all that go, of course.
Even a little chicken....
I can't help it, though:
sometimes, now, even now,
surviving the siege of the world,
I kneel at the altar, my grown daughters
on either side, accept the host in my cupped hands,
and think of one more way to kill that son-of-a-bitch.

Tom Lombardo

Brother Christopher's Boys

Brother Christopher arrived at Gonzaga Catholic
High with Pope John XXIII's reforms
strung on his guitar.

Brother Chris had Brylcreemed hair,
like the James Deans we longed to be,
his penetrating Gallic eyes
two shades of blue.
White collar, frock of martyr black
marked him a Christian Brother,
Order of St. John Baptiste de LaSalle.

We sang for John, both pope and saint.
We sang for Brother Chris.

Juniors, we wrapped ourselves around
his *Kum By Ya*, his Teilhard de Chardin,
his solemn morning meetings
reaching out in prayer to each in private.

Walking on the edge of water,
Chris cast his nets by Christmas.
By Holy Thursday, he pretended
Transubstantiation
with our bread and wine in his hands.
He pulled his nets at Easter.

Snagged, he was excommunicated
Graduation Day. No one told us why.

—hands resting on my thighs,
he leans toward me,
I whiff his Brut, and count his pores—

Recovery From Addiction

I used to go out to walk the dog and forget the dog

—Laurel Blossom

R. G. Evans

Many Feet Going

What they don't tell you
is that it's a tightrope walk
and you will be nude, body
all counterweights and pendulums.
They give you a parasol
(too small, a little frayed),
a bright red nose that makes you easy
to track, and a time limit (too short).
If you find the rope is slack,
that's normal. Keep going.
You're young and strong.
Don't be distracted
by the piles of bones below
(Boob! You thought you were
the first?)—but they are:
waxy winged, chained to rocks,
gnawed through the ribs by raptors.
Your rope has been greased
by the soles of many feet going
one way, all the while
believing they have a choice,
believing they might make it.

Barbara G.S. Hagerty

Visiting Virginia P.

We grow hollyhocks, paint glistening tomatoes,
watch how light fractures a glass of water,
look up words in the middle of the night.
Our bones and narrows rearranged,
we gave birth seven times between us.
Once we followed Berryman,
we were blond disciples
of his cauliflower syntax, his gothic architecture
and small houses, the ruined porch,
the bridge, the truss, the ice,
the freefall into madness.
Nothing could save us
from the gravitational pull of alcohol
until we washed up at AA
among the molded plastic orange chairs,
meetings, coffee, smoke—those were the days
when chain smoking was encouraged
as an antidote to worse things—
among the old timers who spoke in slogans
One Day at a Time, First Things First, Easy Does It.
I thought I'd landed on a planet full of ashtrays
run by an editorial committee of the *Reader's Digest.*
Today you recalled I once said *Pray*
for the unknown help that's already on its way.
Now I meet your son, for the first time, he's 18, grown well
and sturdy, like someone whose boughs we could climb into.

Clinton B. Campbell

Club Soda Nights

It's usually at a party
when I'm holding a watered
down club soda, someone will
politely ask, "How you doin?"
or "What's up?" The smell
of his gin is a bad memory,
tinkling ice cubes cut
into my spine and I blurt out,
"I've been sober 14 years."

It stops meaningful conversation,
the party goers sail
a wide berth around me.
They hide their doubles
in plant stands, get nervous
as if I said I was contagious
and could infect their children.

They look at me as the kind
who drive old cars pasted
with new bumper stickers,
the slick clichés boasting,
"One day at a time"
or "Easy does it."

My wife sees this,
makes a gesture to leave.
She starts with her best friend
tells her, tomorrow is an early day,

promises the hostess she will
call soon, chat, but she won't.

We drive away in silence.
It's times like these
I miss the old days, I want to
put the lamp shade back on my head,
do the bump and grind with
that blond from the steno pool
and call in tomorrow, sick for a week.

She takes my hand, asks if I'm OK,
and we take the long way home.

Iain Haley Pollock

The Straight and Narrow

Near the house that spills banjo music,
the one guarded by a porch stacked

with encyclopedias, ripped out car seats
and outmoded computer screens,

a smell like death stops me. A smell
of slow rot. Across the street, an old man

is mowing his lawn for the last time
before winter, but it isn't the mix

of gasoline and cut grass I smell.
Searching the road for a mashed squirrel

or a drain seeping sewage onto the asphalt,
I find nothing. Nothing at the shotgun house

next door, where the former plot of sickly cabbage
has been uprooted and the soil turned over.

As church bells begin to call out the hour,
competing with the mower's whine, a man—

tattooed face and knit cap worn in all weather—
appears on the porch, wringing the neck of a Miller Lite

in the young morning. I pretend to watch
a stray cat lick a length of calico fur along its spine,

envying the man his public display of freedom, of pain.
A flurry of leaves flies off the overarching maples,

and he tips his bottle at me, then takes a short, sharp swig.
It would be easy to climb the steps and join him,

to spend the day there, trading trips to the fridge
and meandering stories, and some roseate part

of my mind urges my body toward this. That piece of me
remembers rollicking nights in open fields, slurred vows

of happiness, stumbling promises of love,
and cannot understand why we have cast off

such things. That piece—I have to remind it
of the rooms with no windows, of waking

in pools of my own anger and remorse.
I nod back at the man, and head for the corner,

arriving as the bus stops and exhales. My token
chimes into the collection box, and when I find a seat

next to a boy—crowned with headphones
and bopping to a faintly audible beat—the bus

banks away from the curb and into the clear-headed day.

Laurel Blossom

The Intemperate Zone

Hello, I dreamed, and nobody stared. Nobody laughed, though they all had their clothes on. Margo put her arm around my shoulders, *Hi hon*. She drew me behind the green counter. She called to one of the others, who brought a uniform; she helped me into the black and white checked dress with the pretty white starched collar and pretty white starched cuffs on the pretty white capped sleeves. She tied the apron in a white starched bow. She gave me a pair of white socks and black sneakers. They fit. Then she placed a headband on my black and white hair like a white starched crown. It read Happy New Year. She showed me the kitchen. She taught me *whiskey down*.

o

I make circles with my pencil (feather duster) in the air.

I don't know what to do with myself.

I haven't had a drink in two weeks.

o

It's all uphill from here, whispers my dead father in my ear.

o

Still, I thought everything would be changed.

The first time I stayed up past midnight, the first time I stayed up till dawn, the day I got married.

Ah, but my first drink.

o

Please, Freddie said when I tried to give up smoking, *please have a cigarette.*

o

Raise your arm, says Tolstoy.

You think it's free will but it's not. The whole chain of events from the start has led you up to.

Have a drink, said Freddie.

o

If the earth revolves around the sun, if *cogito ergo sum,* if reason reasons only with itself, if chance, if no plan, if whatever happens, that's what it means, if ruled by our subconsciouses, if time equals space, if the world is mostly interstices, if relative, if probably, if we can blow the world to *kingdom come,* if language grumbles to itself alone.

o

In short:

For my eighteenth birthday, I bought myself a cocktail dress.

Martinis rampant on a navy field, embroidered down the side the heart is on.

o

I put glow-in-the-dark tape on the ashtray I used when I smoked in bed.

I may be a drunk, I told Freddie, but I'm not stupid.

o

How I spun from the midnight curve of the piano past the treacherous fountain beneath the stairs, landed just where I prayed I would, leg flung up on the newel post, head back, chiffon trailing on the peacock-feather rug under my bare and toenail-painted pointed foot.

o

I could not keep my eyes open. In the middle of an incomprehensible sentence — the one I myself was speaking — one lid lowered almost completely, the other fallen to the middle of my eye, two yellow eyeballs rolling round like planets, capillaries fizzling out.

The number of bottles of red wine consumed was four amongst six people, three of whom weren't drinking.

Resting my head on the back of my chair, surveying our guests at an angle whereby I could just keep my nose above water.

But not my brain stem.

o

I need help, I said.

What you need is another drink, said my darling Freddie.

o

How liquid, what rapture of the deep.

Makes you believe you can breathe under water.

Sings in your ear: *Take off that tank, your phony mask of oxygen, put on a happy face.*

Now I know what I've got. This must be the bends.

o

The French don't die of arteriosclerosis. They drink red wine.

Like, how you say, zee roto rooter.

What the French do die of is liver failure.

Neverzeeless.

o

Today is my 22nd day without a drink.

Landscape, as in a cartoon, repeats itself.

This truth holds also for wallpaper.

o

Once upon a time, there was a pretty little girl in strawberry curls dressed in polished cotton pink and pinky bows and pampered.

Pearls like rope around her pretty neck.

Whiskers on her chin and whiskey on her breath.

Toss it back, mouth on sleeve, don't need nobody. One o' the boys.

o

I thought I needed more sunshine in the winter. I thought I was depressed.

The doctor recommended I sit every day underneath a *gro-light* for fifteen minutes.

I poured myself a drink. I abandoned my theory.

This may have had something to do with the word *gro*.

What you need is a good night's sleep, said Freddie.

○

March sun steals into frozen gardens, pale fingers on cold skin after too long absence, first slow anxiety of birth.

Makes me shiver.

Water seeps into roots, seeds turn green.

In the maple trees sap like memory begins to push along the veins, liquid feeling of fear these mornings.

I don't want to wake up to.

○

This pervasive, all-encompassing light, said one of my fellow alcoholics.

We were at a meeting.

My limbs were numb. I had to blink several times. It was very, very quiet. I lifted my arm up over my head to shade my eyes. It hurt to lift it.

I thought I was going to see, I wasn't sure, God maybe.

I'd passed out in the middle of the night with all the lights on, blazing.

○

What I needed the next morning was the sound of rice growing.

o

Excuse me, I told the hairdresser, I think my hair's uneven on one side.

He said, how can your hair be uneven on one side. He said he thought I must be drunk. He said, it's either even or it's not.

I said, you either get paid or you don't.

o

There was an incident involving this girl throwing a cupcake in my face when I was ten.

I came home in a depression that over the years I drank to get rid of.

Now I've stopped drinking, the cupcake is back.

o

I used to go out to walk the dog and forget the dog.

o

I was going on a date. My father didn't want me to.

We had a huge fight. I ran out of the house, yelling, Drop dead!

He came after me. He had a heart attack on the driveway.

My mother stood at the top of the stairs.

Now look what you've done, she said. You've killed your father.

o

Once upon a time I had a chipmunk. He liked to nestle in my neck. When I ate dinner, I set him a plate of nuts at the table. They puffed out his stomach and his cheeks.

He always slept with me at night. Sometimes he crawled into the hollow of my back, but I always pulled him out.

One night I came home drunk. I was very drunk. I was fairly drunk. I was totaled.

I fell asleep with my clothes on. The chipmunk must have crawled under the small of my back.

When I woke up the next morning, he was dead. Asphyxiated.

That was the day I knew.

I was never going to have another chipmunk.

o

My husband said he thought the spinach wasn't quite done.

When I looked I saw I'd served it to him straight from the freezer, a hard green brick.

That was the night I knew.

So I tried white wine.

So I tried divorce.

o

Cartographers have a choice, Harry says.

Either distort the size of a continent or change its shape.

o

Two bottles of Wild Turkey, a bottle of Teacher's, a bottle of Canadian Club one shot down, a bottle of Stolichnaya, a bottle of Gordon's Gin, half a bottle of Beefeater's for Peter, an unopened bottle of Ron Rico because nobody seems to drink rum anymore, a bottle of Grand Marnier, a bottle of Metaxa, a bottle of vin santo in memory of Aunt Phoebe, a bottle of saki Gloria gave me who loves sushi, two decanters, one full of Scotch, the other full of brandy, one a wedding present from Freddie's uncle, the other my mother's doughnut-shaped beauty, the last bottle of white wine, three bottles of red, a bottle of Harvey's Bristol Crème.

The sink smelled wonderful.

This is my 34th day without a drink.

o

This is my 34th day without a drink, say I.

There's a pause, an *uh*.

That's wonderful, says Judy.

I don't think I could do that, Gloria says.

You know, you look back over the last month and you try to think of one night when you didn't have a drink and there isn't one, says Peter.

I quit cold turkey a couple of times, says Frank, *but within a couple of months I was saying, oh, I can have a Scotch now and then, and I was back.*

o

I'm not an alcoholic, I don't drink before sundown.

I don't get hung over.

I only drink rosé.

I've never been arrested.

I sleep in Grand Central Station. If I was an alcoholic, I'd be sleeping in the Port Authority.

I ain't dead yet.

o

These, my friends, are the widest latitudes.

o

One day I couldn't find the baby's pacifier. When bedtime came I still hadn't found it. I told him I was afraid it was gone, rolled up in the dirty bed sheets, sent to the Chinese laundry. For good. I kissed him goodnight and hugged him, thinking he'd never be able to sleep.

But he did, he fell asleep. He woke up. He ate, he played, he slept again. I don't get it.

o

Remote areas of New Guinea, for instance, still marked *No Data Available*.

o

Maybe he won't turn out to be an alcoholic. Maybe he's not like me.

o

I used to see Albert in the neighborhood when he was still walking with a cane.

We talked. I thought I was a light unto his darkness.

He called me several times for lunch.

I hated being seen with him, I hated the thought that people might think we were together.

He shook, his clothes were torn, his hair was dirty, stubble in odd patches grew on his cheeks and throat.

I asked him please to stop telling me he loved me.

How are <u>you</u>, I asked, after running out of things to say about myself.

This is life, he shrugged, *it goes on*.

o

Yesterday Albert showed up at Soup Kitchen in the golf cart he uses now for a wheelchair.

We talked. His hand and arm were shaking very badly.

How are <u>you</u>, I asked. *This is life, it goes on*.

o

I was slicing carrots when the phone rang.

Albert said he'd been in love with me for fifteen years.

He said he'd back off but would I have lunch.

I said sure. He warned me I'll be having lunch with a man who is madly in love with me.

o

An azimuthal projection, says Harry, *places one particular point at the center of the map, which is observed from the zenith directly above that point.*

It's my alcoholism, it's my solipsism, it's my alcoholism, it's my solipsism, alcy, soly, alcy, soly, sism sism sism.

o

What you need is a good fuck, said Freddie.

o

Freddie said he was a *functioning* alcoholic.

By this he meant not in spite of, but because.

This is my 65th day without a drink.

o

Ivy on the brick wall, rust red flaring into licks of flame.

Evening sun like a coat of feathers the wind lifts.

Flowers blooming, or not (quite) (yet).

Water about to spill over and over.

I love that.

○

I'm fighting with a stranger, beautiful hair of blue.

Trying to wrestle a beer can from me, a beer can I think is me.

I'm clutching it to my breast.

The angel has his foot in the small of my back, bending.

○

Today is my 90th day.

And what comes after 90? somebody asks.

Everybody answers, *Ninety-one.*

Recovery From Bigotry

*It
was built
to last,
forever*

—Willie James King

Willie James King

Old Cahawba

South, west of Selma
off Highway 22,
on a slab of stone
the name is carved:
Old Cahawba, The First
Capital of Alabama,
and fifty-yards,
maybe more,
at the confluence
of the Alabama river
and the Cahawba river
is a solid plank of iron,
an auction block,
not worn by water,
undefiled by lichen
and time. I
am certain: It
was built
to last,
forever.

Satyendra Srivastava

The Resolve

I watch them
Singing the songs of love
Looking at their tattoos
All those names in them
The Catherines the Elizabeths
The Dianas and Margarets
And then I listen to them
Chanting *Rule Britannia*
And *Pakis go home*
I see them polishing their helmets
Oiling their knives
Demonstrating their kicks on a piece of brick
While looking at me
Etc etc etc
Yet I find myself
On every retreating day
Sitting in the same corner
In the coldest spot
With the resolve to survive
And I survive
And the next morning I get up
Wash
Offer my prayers and
Singing a popular hymn
Go to the shop
Open up the shutter
Switch on the lights
And look at the deposit books
And I feel satisfied

I smile pat my back
Well done son
You'll survive
And I do
And I stay
I hear some of them go
Down under

Georgia Ann Banks-Martin

Montgomery Stairs

The morning sun lends
a gentle glow to this historic
street whose blue markers
offer far fewer words to excise
the ghosts of men marching,
wearing perfectly pointed
white hats, veils draping
their faces and necks, armed
with rocks and hand-made
bombs, taking the homes
of Negroes leaving behind
these sagging stairs
upon which I will not allow
my dog to pee,
something has to be sacred.

Kevin Young

For the Confederate Dead

I go with the team also.

—Whitman

These are the last days
my television says. Tornadoes, more
rain, overcast, a chance

of sun but I do not
trust weathermen,
never have. In my fridge only

the milk makes sense—
expires. No one, much less
my parents, can tell me why

my middle name is Lowell,
and from my table
across from the Confederate

Monument to the dead (that pale
finger bone) a plaque
declares war—not Civil,

or Between
the States, but for Southern
Independence. In this café, below sea-

and eye-level a mural runs
the wall, flaking, a plantation
scene most do not see—

it's too much
around the knees, heighth
of a child. In its fields Negroes bend

to pick the endless white.
In livery a few drive carriages
like slaves, whipping the horses, faces

blank and peeling. The old hotel
lobby this once was no longer
welcomes guests—maroon ledger,

bellboys gone but
for this. Like and inheritance
the owner found it

stripping hundred years
(at least) of paint
and plaster. More leaves each day.

In my movie there are no
horses, no heroes,
only draftees fleeing

into the pines, some few
who survive, gravely
wounded, lying

burrowed beneath the dead—
silent until the enemy
bayonets what is believed

to be the last
of the breathing. It is getting later.
We prepare

for wars no longer
there. The weather
inevitable, unusual—

more this time of year
than anyone ever seed. The earth
shudders, the air—

if I did not know
better, I would think
we were living all along

a fault. How late
it has gotten…
Forget the weatherman

whose maps move, blink,
but stay crossed
with lines none has seen. Race

instead against the almost
rain, digging beside the monument
(that giant anchor)

till we strike
water, sweat
fighting the sleepwalking air.

Tolu Ogunlesi

From a Former Slave to His Ex-Master's Daughter, on Their Wedding Night

This was the house in which I loved you.
In its kitchen, plastic melted against pots
Of fury, and cooled into dreams of smaller work
And kinder beatings.
And this is the love that I had
For you, in a time when pain was cheaper
Than love, and a chain easier
To own than the tiniest slice of cheer.
Those were the times I made salads
From grand ideas, only to flush them
Down the kitchen sink
Into the comforting darkness of a distant underworld.
This was the house in which necessity compelled me
To answer fluently to my brand-new name
Even as I struggled to sing familiar songs
In a tongue stiff from disuse.

Meir Wieseltier

translated from Hebrew by *Shirley Kaufman*

Daddy and Mommy Went to the Movies, Ilana Stays Alone in the Armchair Looking at a Gray Book

She turns the pages, naked uncles
so naked and skinny, run and
even aunties with fannies showing
and others in pajamas as in a show
with yellow cloth stars sewed on.
And everybody so ugly and thin,
and big round eyes like chickens.

It's awfully weird, so gray. Ilana has pencils—red
and blue and green and yellow and pink.
So she goes to her room
and takes all the beautiful pencils
and draws with great flair
glasses and funny faces on all of them.
Especially on that bald skinny boy,
she gives him a big red mustache
and perched at the tip of the mustache—a bird.

Meir Wieseltier
translated from Hebrew by *Shirley Kaufman*

[I saw three baby-faced Germans]

I saw three baby-faced Germans
sitting in Café Notre Dame.
They were so soft in the morning
those three baby-faced Germans,
their field-grass hair
and their barefoot faces.

It rained on the city and the Seine,
washing trash into the gutter,
stale spit and yesterday's headlines,
hitting the Notre Dame and the Seine
and dripping on the eyelashes of passers-by
who moved in an endless line as if weeping
past windows that creaked on their hinges
in front of three baby-faced Germans.

Meir Wieseltier
translated from Hebrew by *Shirley Kaufman*

[The world is full of the righteous]

The world is full of the righteous—
all of us are righteous in our own eyes
drink from our own cups, sit on our own butts
have some pangs of conscience, find our way out
arrange times for meditation, times for tears
lock ourselves in with a little key
and pocket it,
then sleep: and nurture
the shards of our anger.

Randall Horton

Notes From a Prodigal Son # 5

Father,
I needed seasons of dogwood,
the bloom of petals brushing
against an April sky, the way you
taught me to hoop ball in spring.

Yet I also craved wisdom from men
born under the emerald glare of streetlamps,
the aroma of hookers after blue-light sex
running through their heroin nostrils.

Once,
I walked the pearl sand of Eleuthera,
stood in Hatchet Bay's cove—inhaled
salted sea, believed life offered nothing
greater than the Caribbean's blue glass.

I rode the backs of section 8 mules
through customs, not knowing which trip
would be my last, lived runagate style—
free like a prayer from your wife's lips.

Father,
The seeds I planted in those youthful years
have blossomed into a five year sentence,
and it has taken the wring of time's tourniquet
to bring me closer to a life I tried to bury deep.

Richard Garcia

Ballad of Maximum Security

My cellmate's full of bullet holes
and his ear has done a van Gogh.
One bullet hole wants to fly home.
Another bullet hole wants to borrow money
because my cellmate's full of bullet holes
and he needs his tuition for acting school.

He would like to walk past the guards
and right out the front gate, but when he puts on the suit
someone smuggled in, he can't quite pass for a lawyer—
even though he's white he's just a little too white;
and the wind whistling through his bullets holes
makes him appear to be nervous, though he's not.

Me, I want to go to sleep but my dreams
are on vacation and have forgotten all about me.
The guards do laugh when I wonder what my name is.
And Mr. Puppy is having kittens, waiting outside all day
in his boss's limousine. My best friend's Grandma
is picking up the cigarette butts I left on her kitchen floor.

And the door to our cell is doing the electric glide
my fingerprints are spinning whirlpools
the coffee we get once a day has conniptions
and the salt, of which there is none,
is practicing *to be or not to be*
'cause my cellmate's full of bullet holes

and he calls each one by name. One is Mr. Alley.
One is Stella Adler Studio of Acting.

And the guard to our cellblock is up on point
in pink ballet slippers. He says he'll kill us
if we tell anyone about his tutu, the one
with the pick chenille and tiny rhinestones.

And the young murderer next door
doesn't talk much, though if you ask him
who he is, he'll cop to being Mighty Mouse.

Our sad, communal razor is the constellation Ursa Minor,
because my cellmate's full of bullet holes
and his ear is stuck to the wall like a slice of cheese.
Hold your ear up to his ear, and you can hear it——
that chill that brought me here on an open freight car,
that January wind off the Great Lakes, and you
can almost see them, the great jumbled rectangles of ice
piled upon the shore like sculptured coffins.

György Faludy
   translated from Hungarian by *Paul Sohar*

From Farewell to Recsk *(Bucsú Recsktöl)*

We had no pen, no books, to our
depth no news or mail ever sunk,
we had to make do with a mess kit
and one half of a wooden bunk,
we lived with stoolies and slave drivers,
they beat us and kicked us till half gone
from starvation and the shivers
with the lime pit looking on,
seven days a week we worked
and without a hope we went to bed,—
our eyes met in silence saying:
you're too among the living dead.
And yet – what was it in most
of us that kept alive the soul?

***

The suffering. I'd had it coming to me for quite a while.
Had I not surrendered to it, I'd still be an unsated hedonist.
Some were guzzling its cold stream like spring water,
some turned into zombies while others couldn't stop their wails.
Now I am ashamed to say it was easier for me, all my pains
and troubles were numbed when I wove them into poetry.

***

And what is the best part of the lesson?
While erotic desires slowly
abandoned my plundered body

love remained its steady resident.
Zsuzsa became a weightless cloud of silver as she kept
hovering in front of my eyes even when they slept;
amidst constant toil and torture, in the grips of cruel hunger pains
or blind unconsciousness, love remained to fill my veins,
love, the eternal flame that burns but doesn't scorch,
love beyond mere mating urge, beyond the hormones' work,
beyond sex organs' juice
beyond Boccaccio's smirk;
maybe Dante's dream
and Apollo's muse.
Tell Freud for me he is a jerk.

Bette Lynch Husted

Salvage Anthropology

You come to consciousness beside a river roiling
with sharp, tearing teeth. No. They're salmon, pushing
upstream, coming home. You close your eyes again
and when you wake the summer stars are harnessing
the moon to drag it up from scattered clumps of sage.
Tequila. Spring Chinook. And something you've forgotten,
something else. *I really don't know who I am.*

You're not someone who smokes a pack a day, you tell
yourself. The car rolls east as if running away
were possible, as if you could just leave them all.
You drive. A rearview mirror shadow haunts the land
behind you, monster with an appetite for more.
You roll the window down to yarrow, balsamroot
the taste of grief. The funeral over, now you cry.

You know what brought him down, your healer warrior, medic
to brown skin and blood and burning, chopping blades of rage
and alcohol. You learned young: duck and dive. You learned
to take it. *That way madness lies,* they said in school.
How else, then, to survive? And even if you fill Hell's Canyon
with your tears, these dams won't break. That much you know.
What else did Boas and the others save for you to learn?

How will you answer her, your own child: *What's my name?*
she wants to know. *My real name?* You've been working, beading
for her ceremony. But can you give her something you don't
have? It's dark when you turn back toward home
and all that lies ahead. You feel them watching, deer
and coyotes, field mice, things with feathers. You feel the drum
speak from a hollowed place.

Recovery From Loss of Child

*I want
to think of you at fourteen, at twenty-four
or even thirty-one*

—Anthony S. Abbott

William Stafford

A Memorial: Son Bret

In the way you went you were important.
I do not know what you found.
In the pattern of my life you stand
where you stood always; in the center,
a hero, a puzzle, a man.

What you might have told me
I will never know—the lips went still,
the body cold. I am afraid,
in the circling stars, in the dark,
and even at noon in the light.

When I run what am I running from?
You turned once to tell me something,
but then you glimpsed a shadow on my face
and maybe thought, Why tell what hurts?
You carried it, my boy, so brave, so far.

Now we have all the days, and the sun
goes by the same; there is a faint,
wandering trail I find sometimes, off
through grass and sage. I stop
and listen: only summer again—remember?—

The bees, the wind.

Terri Wolfe

Timbuktu

At the end of a year, this is the day
we give each other for having arrived
at this old-growth forest talking about weather,

work, the age of trees—anything but suicide.
I teach his niece to balance
barefoot on stream-slick rocks, how to pretend

leaves placed upon the water are ships
set sail to far-flung places
like Timbuktu. She mouths the word,

the uncertain future, tasting it
over and over, until a snake swims by
her legs, shivery wake of its passing

startling us to dry land, to the yellow feather
she discovers and waves in glee.
At the cars we unfold chairs,

throw faded linen over picnic tables,
make sandwiches, heap plates with potato salad.
I could easily have bought cookies,

instead I ladle strawberries over shortcake, empty
a whole can of whipped cream,
while clouds overhead catch the sunset

and the day begins, bite by bite, to disappear.
Slowly his brother begins to unpack tales
of him, others add their own stories, and

into silence that follows, his father brings
flashlights, a game even the young can play.
Beams glance and collide, spotlight

underbrush and trees, each of us searching
for the eyes of owls and raccoons, whatever
anyone can find glowing in the dark.

J. Stephen Rhodes

This New Never

This new never is quiet enough to fill a hundred caves
with monks. The wind rushes up from our pasture,
bends the pines and brings no news. I whisper
your name and look at your picture on the desk,
the one where you smile like the Little Flower
of Lisieux, willing your pain into someone else's joy,
if only you could decode the mysterious *how.*

You've been gone two months in this new forever
where I can't call you Sunday afternoons
to talk about your last college course, on silence,
a subject we both longed to comprehend and
entered in awkward minutes when we didn't know
what to say from the desert inside, each of us
craving the sound of wind across the mouths of caves.

Some days I swear not to eat. Then you make me break
my vow. You say, in my head, don't be stupid, and I want
to retort, *the way you were,* but don't because you hurt
enough, your eyes tired of looking for I'll-never-know-
what but perhaps a visit with one of your obscure poets
who helped you think yourself to that beach in Mexico
where you sat alone with the black dog watching the surf.

I look for any *ever* or *always* where you might be hiding,
your little girl self leaning out from behind the black oak
in our front yard, you in your pink and yellow dress
playing peekaboo with me. I listen to the sky. In the quiet
you speak: I'm not there, buddy. No dice. But I'm OK.

Gail Rudd Entrekin

Michelle

A woman comes in and joins us for dinner
at the Mexican restaurant, someone's friend,
middle-aged and clearly once a beauty
with slanted green cat eyes and pixie hair.
We're a jovial group, but prone to quiet
moments while we listen intently
to the words someone is speaking.

A young man is talking about disciplining children,
how Berkeley people are so crazy
with fear of abuse that they report spanking
to the police, feel free to reprimand mothers
in public for yelling at their kids who are
tearing around in a store
making other shoppers miserable.
When we laugh, she joins in,
throwing her head back, and the shock
of her laughter is so loud, so cold,
sudden and sharp,
that everyone else stops laughing.

And now she speaks up, tells the story
of a man she saw get out of his van
and beat his child with a belt, how she
called the police, but they didn't come
until after the two had driven away
and nothing could be done for the child.

Finishing the story smiling, she
laughs again, inexplicably, that sudden high loud note

scratching at our hearts. Amid murmurs
and head shaking, we begin to pick up our bags,
gather our coats around us.

Leaving the restaurant, someone
holds the door for her. People fall back
and away, avoiding her circle of despair.
But two women who know she has lost a child,
walk close, their hands gently touching
her back, taking her arms, leaning their
warm bodies into hers.

Mary Jo Bang

You Were You Are Elegy

Fragile like a child is fragile.
Destined not to be forever.
Destined to become other
To mother. Here I am
Sitting on a chair, thinking
About you. Thinking
About how it was
To talk to you.
How sometimes it was wonderful
And sometimes it was awful.
How drugs when drugs were
Undid the good almost entirely
But not entirely
Because good could always be seen
Glimmering like lame glimmers
In the window of a shop
Called Beautiful
Things Never Last Forever.
I loved you. I love you. You were.
And you are. Life is experience.
It's all so simple. Experience is
The chair we sit on.
The sitting. The thinking
Of you where you are a blank
To be filled
In by missing. I loved you.
I love you like I love
All beautiful things.
True beauty is truly seldom.

You were. You are
In May. May now is looking into
The June that is coming up.
This is how I measure
The year. Everything Was My Fault
Has been the theme of the song
I've been singing,
Even when you've told me to quiet.
I haven't been quiet.
I've been crying. I think you
Have forgiven me. You keep
Putting your hand on my shoulder
When I'm crying.
Thank you for that. And
For the ineffable sense
Of continuance. You were. You are
The brightest thing in the shop window
And the most beautiful seldom I ever saw.

Anthony S. Abbott

The Man Who Speaks to His Daughter on Her 40th Birthday
May 8, 2003

1.

"Poetry is the supreme fiction," says Wallace Stevens.
I know. Then how to express the truth, simple
and unadorned as Stevens's "dresser of deal."

You see, I am already equivocating, ducking
behind the decoration of language. So, stop me.
Good. That's better. Now, tell me where you are.

If that's too hard, just tell me——something.
Or appear to me in a dream, or leave a symbol somewhere——
some mysterious talisman that lets me know it's you.

Not the feather floating down trick, that's too common.
Nor bumping around in the old house. Something original
like your name spelled in shells before the tide comes in.

2.

All right, let me try it another way. When you were
three, I let you go to school in the winter without
leggings, without anything to warm your legs.

The teacher told me at the end of the day
and I burned with shame. You were my favorite person;
I was yours. And what I really want to know——

now that all the nonsense about your ghostly reappearance
is out of the way—what I really want to know is
where we would have gone, you and I. I want

to think of you at fourteen or twenty-four
or even thirty-one, want to picture you, know
the clothes you would have worn and how

you would have cut your hair. Early this morning
I walked in the rain to your grave. The tree is gone.
You know I picked the spot because the tree

was there, and now it's vanished like my images
of you. Damn it, anyway. I'm supposed to be
a writer, supposed to create you at twenty-five

or thirty-nine, give you a history. What would
you like? A husband, three children of your own?
A law practice in the suburbs of Boston?

3.

I'm such a romantic fool. That's the problem.
The way I see it, I'm sitting in a tea room
in London, it's raining, of course it's raining.

Umbrella stand inside the door. Dripping coats
hanging on the wall. My hands cupped around
a hot mug of tea. I'm breathing steam. I look up.

There you are, at forty, looking at me with so
much love I feel my body rising from the floor.
You walk over. I try to stand. "No," you say,

"Sit down and rest." You place your hands
on my head and tell me all the years were
nothing—a grain of sand, one grain of sand—

that's all. You tell me you'll come for me
whenever it's right, and then you're gone.
The bell rings, door closes, flash of a heel

And then, nothing but the steady fall of rain.
They look at me, there in the shop, all of them,
and then I laugh and cry, too, I'm sure.

Pretty improbable, don't you think? Wouldn't
sell even in Hollywood, or would it? Still,
dammit, I wish you'd talk to me.

Faye J. Hoops

Parade

As I bedded tulips
Where a sandpile once lay,
A toy soldier popped up in the trowel.
He once climbed hills and marched in parades.
His company commander was one of my sons.

I cradled him in my hand,
Unable to cast him aside.
But there were no hills to climb,
No fortress to guard;
His comrades were scattered or gone.

I stood him up tall
Beside a bulb and pulled the earth
Around him with care.
Each Spring he'll march with the colors
And I'll review the parade.

Annie Finch

Gulf War and Child: A Curse

He is sleeping, his fingers curled,
his belly pooled open, his legs gathered, still
in their bent blossom victory.

I couldn't speak of "war" (though we all do),
if I were still the woman who gave birth
to this soft-footed one: his empty hand,
his calling heart, that border of new clues.

May the hard birth our two heartbeats unfurled
for two nights that lasted as long as this war
make all sands rage, until the mouth of war
drops its cup, this bleeding gift we poured.

Farideh Hassanzadeh

I, I Who Have Nothing

Tonight, without you
this room is like that hospital room
on the bed,
a white sheet
like a cloud, broad,
under it, my small bird
with wounded wings,
nurses mistook
for the corpse of a boy,
his hands
gone with the bombs.
This is why they took you away
from me.
This is why
I didn't see you again.

Do you remember that old song:
I, I who have no one
I, I who have nothing?

When I found you,
you, who were a stray dreamer
among the tic tack followers,
when I found you,
you, who were the act of verse
among the actors of phrases,

I sang my song:
I, I who have my shadow,
I, I who have my shadow-mate.

But tonight, without you
I have nothing but memories,
of my little bird
who exchanged his nest with the wind.

Rachel Tzvia Back

(*their sons my sons*)

Lost limbs again
> this time in a strawberry field

Early morning January sun rises
> gently talks softly to yesterday's
>> rain lingering still at field's edge

where perfect strawberries are ready for eating
> first day of the feast festival of the sacrifice
>> Ishmael taken to the hilltop Issac carried away

This time it is mother Maryam who does not know
> the boys her boys woke early to a school-less day
>> they are racing now through the strawberry field

The red fruit is full sweet with dew and dawn is
> collecting night's blankets day is waiting to spread her
>> arms around us all in the fields and the boys cannot

say how or from where there was no sign a bomb would fall
> in the early morning family field the boys do not know
>> their legs are bleeding their bodies lie still their

limbs are scattered they are half-boys and dead boys
> none of them know how later before the funerals after
>> the hospital Maryam will return to the charred and
>>> beautiful

bleeding strawberry field
> to gather in her scarf scattered flowers
>> and flesh

Rachel Tzvia Back

[When we no longer care]

When we no longer care
   who or how many
are dead
    our own
  running through sprinklers
   in the still
      ablaze
afternoon

when we are too weary
   too hot too bored
     to read even
one more name or
  that day's favorite
tale:

two teenage daughters dead in a day

two bodies on two stretchers
     and their mother
  fallen upon them her mouth
      mangled in open agony
as she strokes their lovely long legs
  now covered in flags

     one more bomb
in a season of many

when we cannot remember the name
      of the smallest baby girl

                carried through narrowstreets
amid crowds of mourners
        curled in her father's arms she is
           tiny

slightest bundle
      of cloth bread wild
              wildflowers
in her father's arms

carried to the graveyard to the crumbling
      edge of driest dirt
           in a season of stray
    bullets

            no one claims someone
                    aimed

when we count our days
      by which bloody "incident"
          killed whose children
in what village or city
      while we travel
          to work
and back home
      and we no longer care

so long as our own
      can still run through sprinklers
              in the late-afternoon
blazing
    heat

Pam Bernard

September 13

time to plant tears, says the almanac
                              —Elizabeth Bishop

Twenty-seven years ago today,
in the Peter Stuyvesant Hotel on West 89th
just off the Park, I handed over sixty
ten dollar bills in a small, white envelope
to a man I had never before met
and was never to meet again.

I don't recall his face, or what he said,
if anything, as he took the money and counted it,
or which knife he used from the table
beside the bed to remove the fetus.
Memory has it limits.

It is enough that the room smelled of the tart,
early apples of September, the ones Sam
the vegetable man hauled on his Tuesday rounds,
bumping down our dirt road
in his wood-sided truck, with baskets
of butternut squash and tomatoes.

How patient the past is,
folded and folded into itself. Look,
a child is waiting for me beside Sam's truck
fingering a button on her cardigan,
her buckle shoes, glistening and fine.

Rebecca McClanahan

Lament

How do I mourn
what barely was—

tadpole legs
swimming my sea,

pulse a muffled
watch's ticking

years too late,
this space that grows

deep below
my girlish breasts,

below my stomach
flat as this day,

flat as the name
stuck in my throat—

Rachel or Hannah
or Anna Kathleen,

my tiny seed,
my never girl.

Sister Lou Ella Hickman, I.W.B.S.

Missing

Told to mourn the child I never had...
I was at a loss. I still am.
There are no words to explain—
Why my childlessness carries no void.
But it is a strange emptiness:
I, a woman, have no desire for a child.
Is this my disability, my loss—a womb denied
The should of femininity which births and nurtures life?
The fact is simple—
There is no goddess within, no wildness,
No jungle tangled with bursting green known as mother.
Today I wonder why; perhaps the words will come.
Surely, the words will come.

Anna Rabinowitz

The Wanton Sublime

Cut to Mary's face
Cut to troubled reeds
　　　Oh my heart is woe, Mary she said so, for
　　　　　　to see my dear son go, and sons I have no more.
Cut to the winding road
Cut to sunrise
Cut to Mary's torso
　　　Oh my heart is woe...
Cut to her finger crooked in his direction
Cut to her thighs
　　　Oh my son, my son who will forsake me.
Cut to her hands on her mons
Cut to her hands on her abdomen
　　　Oh my son, my son must you forsake me?
Cut to winds lowing, hips writhing
Cut to her eyes fixed on definition
Cut to the sky attempting arrival
　　　Oh my son, my son why have you forsaken me?
Cut to fear and wonder and wavering light
Cut to radiance reeking of why
Cut to the gulf between earth and radiance
　　　Oh my heart is woe...
Cut to brittle waves and turbulent seas
　　　of fugitive, turnsole blue
Cut to the magic of disappearance
　　　and the trembling that knows no clemency
Cut and cut and cut again...

Knowing she does not/cannot know
Knowing she is isolate and *sfumato*
    Oh my son, my son why have you forsaken me?

Cut to her soul which is body
    which is the dust
        of an inescapable need

Cut to the garden of her soul which is landmined

Cut to survival

    as possibility
        as mark...

FOR THOSE WHO ARE TO COME

    That I have been...

    That I have...

    To remind...

        My life...

        LIGHT NOT BE EXPLAINED

Recovery From Divorce
or Loss of Lover

Light is falling
through the windows of my half-empty house

—David Bottoms

David Bottoms

In a U-Haul North of Damascus

1:

Lord, what are the sins
I have tried to leave behind me? The bad checks,
the workless days, the Scotch bottles thrown across the fence
and into the woods, the cruelty of silence,
the cruelty of lies, the jealousy,
the indifference?

What are these on the scale of sin
or failure
that they should follow me through the streets of Columbus,
the moon-streaked fields between Benevolence
and Cuthbert where dwarfed cotton sparkles like pearls
on the shoulders of the road? What are these
that they should find me half-lost,
sick and sleepless
behind the wheel of this U-Haul truck parked in a field on Georgia 45
a few miles north of Damascus,
some makeshift rest stop for eighteen wheelers
where the long white arms of oak slap across trailers
and headlights glare all night through a wall of pines?

2:

What was I thinking Lord?
That for once I'd be in the driver's seat, a firm grip
on direction?

So the jon boat muscled up the ramp,
the Johnson outboard, the bent frame of the wrecked Harley
chained for so long to the back fence,
the scarred desk, the bookcases and books,
the mattress and box springs,
a broken turntable, a Pioneer amp, a pair
of three-way speakers, everything mine
I intended to keep. Everything else abandon.

But on the road from one state
to another, what is left behind nags back through the distance,
a last word rising to a scream, a salad bowl
shattering against a kitchen cabinet, china barbs
spiking my heel, blood trailed across the cream linoleum
like the bedsheet that morning long ago
just before I watched the future miscarried.

Jesus, could the irony be
that suffering forms a stronger bond than love?

3:

Now the sun
streaks the windshield with yellow and orange, heavy beads
of light drawing highways in the dew-cover.
I roll down the window and breathe the pine-air,
the after-scent of rain, and the far-off smell
of asphalt and diesel fumes.

But mostly pine and rain
as though the world really could be clean again.

Somewhere behind me,
miles behind me on a two-lane that streaks across

west Georgia, light is falling
through the windows of my half-empty house.
Lord, why am I thinking about this? And why should I care
so long after everything has fallen
to pain that the woman sleeping there should be sleeping alone?
Could I be just another sinner who needs to be blinded
before he can see? Lord, is it possible to fall
toward grace? Could I be moved
to believe in new beginnings? Could I be moved?

Janet Winans

In Tule Fog

In retrospect it all makes perfect sense, though at the time,
no foreshadowing. A summons to jury duty arrives
in a plain envelope, #10, behind a cellophane window,
return address, Capitol Office Building, Federal Court.
Report on Monday, January 4 at 9 A.M., Courtroom B.
Attached, directions to the parking structure, Level 3
adjacent to the courthouse; enclosed, green 1-day pass.
"Lock vehicle. Leave pass visible on dash."

Sacramento, an hour's drive at least from where she lives
and more, with tule fog as thick as wool in wintertime.
She leaves home in the dark, headlights reflected back,
yellow foglights dim, irrelevant. For miles on 99 she shadows
semis hauling sugar beets or hay until the city separates itself
from mist, the streets she peers at turning recognizable.
The trial may be long, they're told, although not newsworthy;
a bank somewhere was robbed, suspect, alleged, in custody.

So the frigid month proceeds. She drives each morning
in the wet and dark, courtroom gripping her imagination.
Judge and lawyers, jurors turn three-dimensional, familial,
defendant shape-shifting somehow into someone known.
Evenings she starts home again just as the fog returns,
enfolds her car, a quiet capsule moving in its private space.
Somewhere in this shrouded place her world is altering.
She will end a marriage and reclaim her life.

Stellasue Lee

Change of Season

I've not wanted to leave the house lately.
I've been content as grass growing,
wild with color
and deeply rooted
as an old tree with new growth for spring.

I long for nothing—
dream of just where I am,
worry over the indoor plants,
and the camellias coloring the front porch,
the roses gathering strength from winter.

Oh, did I mention the coyote
walking down the middle of the road
at four in the afternoon yesterday?
And that I woke to rain today?
Did I tell you that I put a log in the fireplace

and when the embers turned bright orange,
I added all the court papers,
all but the final decree,
and watched as the whole thing went up?
They burned bright as a sunny day.

Alexa Selph

Leavings

Let me leave you
    with the wish that someday
        your leaving me

will find its way
    into your own
        mixed bag of regrets,

along with the unexpected
    notice of insufficient funds,
        the plate of food removed

while you were still hungry,
    the poem you've always wished
        you could write.

You I will scrape
    carefully into my compost
        heap, along with a few

potato skins, some used coffee grounds,
    a little leftover chopped broccoli
        (gone bad), and some broken eggshells.

Next spring I'll feed you
    to my daylilies, after
        my memories have had time

to shift and turn,
    decay and change
        into something rich and good.

Dennis Ward Stiles

Bringing You Back

I drag your shadow behind me
on a long string. It catches
on curbstones and bumps across

November's brittle leaves. I bend
over your footprint in the bedroom
and gaze along the trail
of promises you left.

Your sleep still fills the mirror.
Your laughter warped my cheekbones.
Your chin

built a nest in my shoulder.
When I am drunk, the rabbit by the bed
tells me how quiet you've become

how you've gone from pen and ink
to watercolor. My dreams leave
traces light as lace. I wait in corners

for your outline to appear
for you to whisper something
about love or licorice.

I have a sketch of us
you've never seen.
You're made of midnight.
I'm all squint.

Rebecca McClanahan

First Husband

After the marriage exploded, it sifted
down to this: the scar your fist left
on the filing cabinet where I kept my poems,
and on the ironing board stacks of Army khakis
whose pleats never flattened to your satisfaction.
It helped to think of you that way, a detonation
searing my eyes from everything but the white flash
that lit my path years later to a place
where I was still young enough to pass
as a bride. I've kept you hidden, even my friends
don't know. And I had almost buried you
when the Christmas card came—your fourth wedding,
complete with children acquired along the way.
Your chest has dropped, and gone completely
is the hairline that began its early retreat
when you were still the boy I would marry.
Your shirt is wrinkled; beside you
the new wife is already starting to fade.
Something in her chin reminds me of me. I send
my best wishes. For finally after twenty years
a memory ripens and falls into my lap:
our last trip, a Canadian forest
where strange animals destined for extinction
roamed the green hills. At a roadside stand,
we stopped for melons. Later, you steered
with one hand, and all the way down the mountain
I licked the sweetness from your fingers.

Rebecca McClanahan

Never, Ever

                         What I thought
I could never forgive
now salts the mustached
edge of his lip

Not the act   I will never…

                         But his hunger

for a mouth new
as a wife's
can never be

a mouth (I later learned
begging for details)
tinged with the taste
of tobacco and Scotch

Oh to be the bad
woman for someone

How good I would taste

                         And the buzz

he must have felt
the insect whirring
in his brain   the approach
of wings   the landing

But it was worth it
wasn't it my friend asks

I mean   now that you're
back together and better

She says it the way
the sighted make heroes
of the blind   the way
we believe amputees
grow suddenly noble

She says it
in a hungry way like she really
needs to know

                              the taste   the buzz

my friend whose husband
would never   Could
never

Rebecca McClanahan

The Other Woman

In dreams I always love her.
We sit shaded
beneath big hats,
sipping mint tea, laughing.
I admire the flame
of her hair, the delicate
freckled wrist.

We ask small questions:
Did he always fold his towel
just so, over the banister?
Do Wednesdays still
knit his brow?
Her pale stockings
rub together.
Her voice, torn lace.

Across our faces
sun weaves
a lattice of
shadow and light.
We sit shaded
beneath big hats,
asking small questions,
nodding.

Renée Michele Breeden

Original Sin

i can't deny
i felt safer in the cusp of your arms than any place else
and i loved myself with every one stroke
of your fingers through my hair
i love you man…and there isn't enough self-expression
to define the depression of 10 years
of loving someone in silence, the way i loved you
but there are some things
our love couldn't get us past,
some things we should have never asked, or told
you promised to have & to hold her
and i die every time i think of that ill-fated romance
& how it has me in a state of continual compromise
& oh the lies i told myself
so that i was clear to love you
poet that i am
i used my pen to write you scarlet letters
cause there could be no shame
in wearing this love on my chest
but the ink defiled my bed
and instead of loving myself enough, i let you love me
and compromised God's plan
see i believed we couldn't be beautiful again
if we did not take this chance,
if we did not grab a hold
of this infinite desire…but the fire is too hot this way
an inferno burns from the inside out—
and i cannot get burned again…
this sin is consuming me
never intended to be the other woman

Ellen Doré Watson

Yes From No

When I decided not to drive my car clear through
    her new house and instead to look in, I saw
two place mats and oh the dinners he will make,
    saw the cookbooks wrenched out of my kitchen,
the sesame oil set back on the shelf empty, unthinking,
    the reason I scold him, the reason he's leaving,
the reason next time I drive by she's on the porch
    as if waiting for a man with suitcases to drive up,
my man, the gone one whose body still sleeps
    downstairs, and I also saw a dog I didn't like,
first mean, then goofy with its bone and drool
    at the back door grinning up like a goddamn
trained seal, but god help me I was for a minute
    demented—no, a screenwriter, pondering the ways
to kill a dog, send a little message, yes—in the movie
    version when I drive through her house, her dog's
exactly in my path, and I bust him through to the other
    side—how easily everything turns to slapstick or gore,
but in real life what punishment is there for this sin or that,
    my many omissions while they committed and
committed. I'm beginning to think the only punishment
    that counts is the kind handed down from the forehead,
handed up via reflux, finding its way somehow to set forever
    between the ribs like a kind of stitch, one in a line
of crooked stitches poorly sewn by our own child-hands
    because we used to know yes from no, sin from sin,
maybe it was the child in me that decided not to drive
    straight through them, the grown-up that said
go home and eat a pot of rice and get silly with my girl.

Thomas Lux

Criss Cross Apple Sauce
—*for Claudia*

Criss cross apple sauce
do me a favor and get lost
while you're at it drop dead
then come back without a head
my daughter sings for me
when I ask her what she learned in school today
as we drive from her mother's house to mine.
She knows I like some things that rhyme.
She sings another she knows I like:
Trick or treat, trick or treat
give me something good to eat
if you don't I don't care
I'll put apples in your underwear ...
Apples in your underwear—I like that more
than Lautremont's umbrella
on the operating table, I say to her
and ask her if she sees the parallel.
She says no but she prefers the apples too.
Sitting on a bench
nothing to do
along come some boys—p.u., p.u., p.u.
my daughter sings,
my daughter with her buffalo-size heart,
my daughter brilliant and kind,
my daughter singing
as we drive from her mother's house to mine.

Joseph Mills

Recipes

On Sunday, he cooks for the week,
shopping in the morning
and spending the afternoons
listening to the Oldies station
chopping vegetables, frying chickens,
baking casseroles
until the kitchen is filled with steam,
and condensation thickens each wall
so that when he steps onto the back porch
to lower another finished dish
into the freezer
the air seems cool, even chilly,
and as the heavy lid closes,
forming a seal,
for a moment,
he feels safe.

Sometimes, he still forgets
to cut the recipes in half,
and he stacks "her" portions
in the back corners.
If she returns,
she can excavate there
determine from his diet what he felt,
and perhaps she'll recognize
in those rising layers
of meals, those weekly cycles
of emotions getting smaller
and simpler,

how he tried to train himself
to forget her,
but how something
always remained,
prepared and frozen,
waiting to be eaten.

Liesl Jobson

Missive From Shakaland

She held this Zulu Love Letter, my daughter, wound about
and through her fingers, parallel strands of tiny beads: blood
coloured leading into a bold geometry. Unwittingly she bought
an orange-blue-white message of the old South African flag.

She did not know the fragrances contained in this souvenir
were the scents of my childhood—whiff of sweet grass,
sugarcane fields, snuff, woodsmoke. Tied on my nanny's
back I learned them, ingrained in Ma'Msomi's Vaselined hands.

Now like angry teeth, these beads click on my desk
I am too afraid to wear this fragile thread, with black eyes
strung on a cheap filament, quickly, by a Zulu mother
with hungry mouths to feed, Ma'Msomi's tribal cousin.

It was the month of the divorce, my daughter's school trip
to Eshowe to study the ancient arts of stick fighting,
spear carving and shield making—she saw a *Sangoma*
throw the bones. She recognised, she said, the war dance.

Each night counting these glass fragments under my fingernails
I remember Ma'Msomi's valley where AIDS swallows
children, spits up mounds of rusty earth without headstones
and try to remember that custody battles are not terminal.

I hold this delicate dispatch tonight and recite the colours learned
at Ma'Msomi's knee: black for sadness, blue for hostility,
orange for withering away, white for good luck, red for passion.
Her necklace gift whispers, "The sun will rise again tomorrow."

Deborah P. Kolodji

[lingerie drawer]

lingerie drawer
after the divorce
skimpier

Aimee Nezhukumatathil

Small Murders

When Cleopatra received Antony on her cedarwood ship,
she made sure he would smell her in advance across the sea:
perfumed sails, nets sagging with rosehips and crocus
draped over her bed, her feet and hands rubbed in almond oil,
cinnamon, and henna. I knew I had you when you told me

you could not live without my scent, bought pink bottles of it,
creamy lotions, a tiny vial of *parfume*—one drop lasted all day.
They say Napoleon told Josephine not to bathe for two weeks
so he could savor her raw scent, but hardly any mention is ever
made of their love of violets. Her signature fragrance: a special blend

of these crushed purple blooms for wrist, cleavage, earlobe.
Some expected to discover a valuable painting inside
the locket around Napoleon's neck when he died, but found
a powder of violet petals from his wife's grave instead. And just
yesterday, a new boy leaned in close to whisper that he loved

the smell of my perfume, the one you handpicked years ago.
I could tell he wanted to kiss me, his breath heavy and slow
against my neck. My face lit blue from the movie screen—
I said nothing, only sat up and stared straight ahead. But
by evening's end, I let him have it: twenty-seven kisses

on my neck, twenty-seven small murders of you. And the count
is correct, I know—each sweet press one less number to weigh
heavy in the next boy's cupped hands. Your mark on me washed
away with each kiss. The last one so cold, so filled with mist
and tiny daggers, I already smelled blood on my hands.

Recovery From Loss of Innocence

We lose our innocence believing
—Kurtis Lamkin

Kurtis Lamkin

We Lose Our Innocence

We lose our innocence believing.
Arrival begins the great festival of loss.
Just when we realize the mystery is the beauty
it's time to go.

We swam the daylight stone cerulean
sea pulling men pulling sea pulling men
we wrestled from the cold deep
a huge fur blob, dragged it upshore by its harpoon.
Young legs came running
"it's a whale, it's a whale!"
Kumana said, "the fisherman …"
I pronounced it the ocean's
wicked sense of humor, promise
determined to remain promise.
Folonko squatted, stroked the wet fur
faced the blue west and said,
"this is murder."
I thought we were calling it what we wanted
if we have to call it what it is
let me confess my split dilemma:
I swim terrible.
So why did I challenge the roiling sea?

Desire calls her lover, *my heart*.
Hunger names him an organ lower:
vulva, labia, clitoris – such music
a man should never be ashamed of his vagina
he's pushed into this world to pay the gamble

that a fetus took
at his best he pays and plays without excuses
otherwise, he's just a flunkie
dumping his period on the flunkie next
(you have to see this through the eyes of the number-crunching moon:
     The whole world bleeding.
     The whole world bleeding.)

I was drowning in the distance and the deep.
I called the fur-thing my buoy and held on.
By surviving, I lost my innocence believing
it had to be dead to save me.

C. C. Thomas

Sacred Water

I lost my virginity
in Yenowine Creek.
It was not the combining
that remarked it
for I knew that was fleeting.
The reverence was in the water.
My legs, pried apart,
felt the cool ticklish trickle
as I saw the overhead sunlight
dapple on his hair
causing a patchwork
of auburn, so that,
for a moment,
his face was unrecognizable,
and then the blood,
in a soft pool,
finally eddied, swirled
and washed away.

Barbara Presnell

Where They Come From, Where They Go

Florence Crittendon Home, Lexington, Kentucky

Word's out: Tina's
run off in the night,
taking only
what she carries inside:
her baby wrapped tight
and warm in her belly,
a head full
of memories
she's too young to know are best
left behind, a few vague plans
she'll follow like stars.
No matter she can't read
the words on this page,
or her child won't know
the face of its daddy
any better than she does.
If there's money for cigarettes,
she'll get by,
for the night is an arm
around her shoulders,
the night's the dark womb
of the mother who loves her.
Back at the home girls
press big stomachs together
and stare through the panes
for a shadow of Tina.
While they box up her
clothes, put clean sheets

on her bed, Tina curls
like a child in the lap
of the fog,
the streetlight a halo,
gone by morning.

Naomi Ruth Lowinsky

on the anniversary of my first marriage

had i never leapt across the yellow grasses

of that meadow near Point Reyes to the sound

of the Hallelujah chorus   never wound my adulterous

legs around my flute playing lover   never been so blatant

so lewd   i might still be married to that boy

from high school   still be small and hidden in the pocket

of his green corduroy jacket   peering out at other people's

lives   had I never danced to the bongos and the setting

sun at Big Sur   never almost run away with that ferryman

masseur who could transport me to the land

of naked bodies and temple whore lore   had i never been

such a bitch such a floozy   never danced topless

in a bar   never known the lotus flower

to blossom in my own goddess body   never lived alone

with three children   fed them eternal

soup of the week   never been apprenticed

to a witch   studied spells and incantations   never sat on a wooden

floor howling with what came to me out of a cave   never seen yellow

bellied death sitting on my bed forcing me to face

my real life— get up wash face bring fever down   stay alive to raise the children—   would i have found my place   in this sweet

bed   where wanton and wild are loved by a man

who has light in his eyes   where tigers and lions roam   yellow hills

in my dreams   and both sun and moon shine on me?

Jericho Brown

Because My Name Is Jericho

You would not believe me if I told you
       I met a man called Joshua.

I am not a city nor a saint.
       He knew where my body had been.

I named each place. Then after a long silence
       He played a song for me on his trumpet.

There is a word

       You will not have me say. So my mouth plays
Now as it did then, open,

       The broken bell of a tossed horn—
Each eye, my entire body, struck

       Open, dry
As it was that night. And maybe you're

       Right. Something had to be taken
From me. I was too beautiful

       To be such a sinner. He must have hated me
For that. Maybe some of us are

       Better broken into—we mend
Easy as a ripped shirt or

A damaged wall.
If ever asked about damage I will tell

What I tell myself. I am overwhelming.
He was overwhelmed

See. I am just as much a man
As Joshua. I've got the silence to prove it.

Therése Halscheid

Peasants Around Small Fires

along the Volga River, Russia just after Communism

flames orange their eyes

           the life inside
           worn faces

 one, cooking slim fish,
manages a silenced name—

     God

he says
with frightened pleasure

God   and again
  God

     like so, like that
     while waters came

the current language of water there
              at their boats
       moored
     to the trees
  by the banks of Yaroslavl

God   with winds letting loose
         against evening

pushing
a slow mist upon everything —

God   he continues
      God

until they stand, they all sing
      barely seen

               unsecreting

        the new sound of their bodies.

Becky Thompson

Post-Attica Visit

I dreamed there was a jungle gym
                     in your cell, we
trapezed from side to side
                     limber and flying
the guards heard laughter
                     and came running
we made ourselves tiny birds
                     on the metal tree top
our wings small enough to squeeze
                     through the bars
into the meadow the sky so blue
                     you lost your breath
we flew until just before count
                     squeezed back in
I see blue birds now and yearn, I
                     sleep sitting up

John McAllister

Dog Days

It was a row, a humdinger.
In the end the young bride damned
her marriage to hell, called the dog
and caught the train home to mother.

Which row it was she never said.
But she was always shifting furniture
so perhaps it was the time he got home from work
and went from bath to bedroom in the dark.

He gave her a few days, until it was plain
her temper would last as long as her red hair,
before he appeared at the door.
He said, *I've come for the dog.*

Cathy Smith Bowers

The Love

The love that ended yesterday in Texas
crawled out of the sea
fresh-eared and barnacled,
his lashless eyes astonished
at the shook-out world
where nothing swayed or rippled
but stood one-minded and dry,
pointing forever upward.
He dressed
and boarded a slow boat
that kept him centuries adrift,
finally jumping ship
in a country shaped like a lobster,
the claws of its faraway shores
reaching out to him.
There his journey continued
like the long, slow haul
of a glacier, over mountains,
through gorges and canyons,
across prairies where
ghosts of Indians
whispered his many names.
To the edge of the desert
where he bought a hat
and mounted the horse
that brought him here

to this honky-tonk,
to the corner near the jukebox
where he sits
mourning the woman
whose voice, like the sea,
still calls him.

Recovery From Illness or Injury

All the scars will heal one day

—J.E. Pitts

J. E. Pitts

Scar Inventory

You look like a victim of a shark attack, a friend said,
when I took my shirt off during a long tennis match.
It was deep summer, and
I was two months out from the knife.
It's true that from my collarbone down, the
white lines and bumps are the trail of
procedures recommended,
agreements reached, waivers signed in
the transactions of the flesh.
A slice here, a slice there,
they cut down through the sack we call the skin—
clamps are applied, what needs to be done is done,
then the stitch machine sews things up in a snap.
Others are not so blatant—
the goofball emergencies, clumsy days and nights.
The long one on the back of my right leg
where I slid down a ladder as a boy.
The car accident, where I broke my ankle
and a steel screw binds the delicate shattered bones.
The bicycle wreck, where the
pedal's serrated edge came down
and almost sliced an Achilles tendon.
The high school fight at the skating rink,
where a class ring dug across my eyebrow.
Such an autobiography.
All the scars will heal one day—
at least that's what the doctors say.

William Greenway

Eurydice

When my wife woke from four months
of coma after a "massive" stroke,
with chances of recovery "minimal,"
and we had finally flown home
in a tiny jet around the polar horn
of Swansea, Cardiff, Reykjavik, Goose
Bay, Toronto, Cleveland, Youngstown,
I sat by her wheelchair in a class
like a kindergarten where kids of all ages
cut colored cloth, stacked blocks,
and pieced puzzles like a map
of the world. When they shook their heads
to lament how she couldn't remember
anything or speak, I wrote
on a big pad in crayon, "Let us go
then you and I."

After she had read it aloud,
she went on in her whispery voice
to chant, eyes closed, the rest
of the poem from memory while
the rehab staff in their green
and blue scrubs gathered around
and stood open-mouthed as something
odd and unintelligible, yet
somehow strangely familiar,
came to them from a far place,
deep and dark where she had been,
beyond the reach of light and love
and even words themselves.

Susan Varon

Poem to My Right Hand

Alien one that I am learning
        to make my god,
you are beautiful
in your attempts to return
to your destiny, As in, *human*
As in, *making fire.*

When you succeed in grasping
the glass I want to drink from,
my thirst intensifies
while you draw it closer, closer.

Things I have taught you to pick up:
the candle (unlit)
the silver bell
the matchbox

I am trying to retrain you to know
        your nature,
to be proud of what you can do.
I believe in the new pathways
the brain is forging itself,
the alternate Rube Goldberg connections
        around the dead matter,
I can see them, hear the voices
of instruction and encouragement,
the brain talking to itself while it does
        its work.

In a notebook I practice the new penmanship,
submitting to the spasms that wildly jig
                    the pen,
breathing into the letters emerging new and wet,
every one
                    worth fighting for.

Shaindel Beers

A Study in Weights and Measures

She punches ruthlessly—like the women at the gym
who've taken kickboxing,
but there's something different, so I ask who she's hitting,
and she says "Cancer," and I wish I knew how to fight
because when I first heard the word in relation to myself,
I thought *God, at last a rest*, and pictured a few months of time alone
to think and read and sleep in,
perhaps so long that I would feel ready to again take on the burden
of this world that has become so heavy in so short a time
that I don't know why people fight back to carry it even longer—

except there's still a lot I want, things that may seem silly.
Climb Mt. Brown (elevation 7487 ft) though it's just a hill
to people who've climbed Everest or Kangto or Antofalla, because I'm ashamed
I made it only halfway, a testament to my lack of discipline—just like
my meager writings which I held next to my *Complete Works of Keats*,
who died only one year older than I when my diagnosis came from the doctor.
This all seems panicked, looking back a year later,
but now, all tests negative, there's the bleeding
again, appointment three days away, and my head feels as light
as the balloon I let go in Mrs. Chamberlain's kindergarten class
with my name and address tied to the string
so that someone would write back to tell me how far it went—
maybe to Ohio or Kentucky, depending on the speed
and direction of the wind.

And though the test seems so close, there's so much
blood I wonder if, like that balloon, I'll lose my grounding,
float away like that red speck—smaller, smaller, gone.

Genie Cotner

Ikebana

She chooses a branch, grass, stones
a few blossoms,
a leaf with a hole

where an insect has eaten.
She is learning.
                    Form and empty space.

Heaven, earth, and man—
in the Kyoto temple, the offering
of flowers to the spirits of the dead.

    She remembers a man from Maintenance
standing at her office door years ago.
He had heard she was sick.

Heard it was cancer. A gentle man,
he didn't know much English,
didn't know her well.

In Japan, I knew a woman who had that—
the same kind.
                She died, he said.

Their eyes met. She nodded.
She understood,
                lived.

Marcia Slatkin

A Late Blessing

I wake her
with touch, rubbing
her shoulders, telling
the time.

My hug fills
the curve of her chest,
arms circling warmth
through her length.

When she cleans dishes,
I reach to fill the kettle
by nudging her cheek
with my forehead,
then snuggling, and hearing
her squeal.

Despite grease
on her face at sleeptime,
I kiss her, wish her
good dreams.

This is the mother I battled
when young; the mother
who beat my defiance;
the one I hit back.

While we walk now,
she gives me her hand,
its back veined and grizzled—
but its wondrous palm
soft as persimmon,
warm and trusting
as a child.

David Bottoms

A Daughter's Fever

Dark ivy draws a wave across the yard,
even the shadows
are streaked with rain. Light drizzles the oak leaves
and I rock behind this screen,
listening to squirrels, the bickering of jays.
The five a.m. garbage truck
doesn't wake you
as it scrapes the curb from can to can.
Three hours of crying lit the windows next door,
but now you lie as quiet
as the rain. After the dozen books,
the trail we frayed from piano
to puppets, to the cardboard frog
on his pond of cut wool,
I lean to your blanket
and hold my breath.

Rachel, about the little girl
who started home late
across the darkening woods…
Someday I'll give you the words I used all night
to guide her home. So many ways
to enter the forest and never return.
But happily that's another ending.

Under a basket of cornflowers
hung from the mantel,
she sleeps now in her cottage near the town.
Her father watches

new light clothe the trees.
In his orchard
the crows out-cackle the squirrels.
He holds his breath to hear
her breathe, around his finger
small fingers curl.

Barbara Mitchell

Boy of Silence

in the beginning there was my son
a ceremony of such small proportion
he arrived in a swath of silence

i waited for his song
but his voice was a trapped bird in the throat
he grew to a pale shadow
eyes smudged to neutral
he filtered my comings and goings in half-tones

i copied the form of my lips
over and over against his ear
but his teeth clamped tight
against the easy slur of speech

he never came out of his silence
leaned instead to the quieter syllable
that scribbled its reason inside his head

i prayed for transparency
for his skin to thin to a clear hue
a window to see what passed for words
through his blood

i waited for understanding
to learn why he traced his hearing against mirrors
laid his face flat against windows
perhaps he felt small in the midst of such big hours
soothed himself by finding definition against reflection

perhaps the world was too noisy for him
he huddled

one long leg bent up and up over the other
sometimes he curled backwards
the contortions he went through to find peace

he would sit for hours
take part in the sun's departure
watch its round face
a brilliant wound
slip over the edge of the earth
and all movements of him were still
his eyes fixed
i'm sure he bears the scar of every sundown

in the end there is only my son
and all my grief sharpened to love
a pulse of joy flares in his heart
and his eyes unbutton to the glory of a new dawn
even as he pulls a sigh from the ordinary day
he is reaching for me
teaching me to celebrate in the space between words

he dances through hours
his lips a pressed secret
brightness curved to a mood that swings inside him
perhaps a music maker resides in his limbs
for he spins and sways
hands braiding the air
themselves
they swipe at laughter dangling in open space
i'm sure i see it enter his face

in the end
there is only my son
and with our hands joined
together we are fluent
in our composure
of silence

Joan Houlihan

Devon's Treatment

I.

Desolate and bound, we rose, guided
                    by random signs skeining his retina

and hemisphere's capacity for syntax

appraised his worth, his known abrasions gone
dayside to a pewtered space

                    where all the higher latitudes poured south.

Odd-postured,
         pale
                face tainted,
made nothing in a cold gown

he was bathed in
                    curative allure

whose practitioners fostered his waking—

Talk through your fingers. Make yourself known.

On opening the crown
                    they found the chakra scribbled

and dense

flashed "devon"

　　　then "arm"

　　　　　(right hand pointing, left hand still)

saw him move his jaw and blink—

　　　an *ignis fatuus* of speaking.

Often we were advised
the "self" may have come loose,

　　　the spark snapped out,

gone dark to probing

　　　and every place a ruin.

II.

　　　It wasn't sleep we got,
　　　just something we walked in,

　　　a stoppage, then palmward, the hands.

No alternate pleading, no divinations.

We saw the ritual through.

With summer's shade swallowed,
we took him home

　　　an unexpected structure,

　　　his aurora quiet, his single source of speaking

a new corona

                    around which false memories

circled to be torn up daily,

musculatures, by heating,
            were drawn to return.

You are no comfort, make comfort, he said

believed himself into an airport

                        preparing for departures

as our hand-held ministrations gave way to

small breeze-strokes of leaf-fall,
                        fast beauty and the rustle that dispels it

shaky light along new ground,
            and the length of one step braced.

Jenni Meredith

Vertical Blinds

Between each vertical
Thin slits of sun
Illuminate my clouds;

Each day I move the
Cord a little further and
The slits grow wider.

Alexa Selph

Therapy

I moved among nests of sleepy fish,
tunneling through a netherworld
of broken bottles and rusty cans.

After a few million years,
I began to walk on land, nuzzling
the ferns as they dropped their spores to the wind.

Glaciers formed, and I grew fur,
developed small hands. Foraging
by night, day by day I learned
to form words and draw pictures.

I named my friends and family,
told stories known only to me,
sharing a dish of truth warmed over.

When finally I found myself
naked in my skin, no circles
around my eyes, I returned to the water

and saw that from this side,
on a windless day, the surface is smooth.

Rhett Iseman Trull

Counting Miracles at the State Asylum

Some nights, Estelle lets us join her outside
while she takes a smoking break
and calls her girlfriend on her cell phone.
Josh and May and I sit nearby in the grass,
leaning against each other, counting miracles.
Not white doves drifting by at just the right moment
or some former comatose staggering back from the brink,
making talk-show claims about light. We don't believe
anymore in that rare luck some call blessing.
But we've learned a thing or two
about miracles for the common man,
the stuck man: a nest of robins about to hatch;
fast cars on the highway, going somewhere;
in the sky, webs of lightning. And that squirm of rhythm
whenever the stars flare up, holding on
to centuries of wishes, polishing them
over and over. The stars know the danger
of even a bingo-paced Wednesday
and light themselves every night in celebration
of the simple fact of our survival.

Pramila Venkateswaran

Praying for Miracles at Velankani Amman's Shrine, Tamil Nadu

I stand with mother in a weary line winding through
a dusty courtyard into the church doorway,
my right fist tightening around a one-inch brass
foot I picked out from masses of metal organs
displayed in slotted tin trays. Knee problem,
murmurs a graying woman, wiping perspiration
from her face with the end of her sari, a joint
shining in her palm. *Velankani amman, take care of me,*
each utters, under the cool roof of the steeple,
dropping messages with chosen limbs or organs
into a box at the altar's foot. Hands folded,
we kneel on the cool floor, spires of prayers
rising from our mouths to mingle with the incense.
Our eyes drink in the Virgin's blessing. Outside,
crows from mango pews caw ceaselessly.
The pain in my foot nags like their tireless cry.
I meet Velankani Mary's tranquil gaze above
the pleats of her garment, each like the fold
in my left foot where stitches forced skin and skin to mesh.
I look at the brass in my palm, neat and whole,
unlike the ravine with a twisting stream in my foot.
If the marring of my flesh brings me here,
then this is how a goddess stitches me to her,
making me whole.

Diane Holland

At Baggage Claim

When a cooler you'd expect for a picnic,
out of place in the scramble of black bags,
when that bright cask is labeled *human
eye tissue,* you might blink, as I did,
my body remembering itself fragile.

How I've taken for granted the fretwork
and wizardry holding me tethered
for now, never thinking of my self as
interchangeable or that some orphan part
of me might one day go alone.

Consider that small and splendid gauze,
curved to mound like a gossamer tussock:
what sly moments streamed through
in a shiver of cells, its luminance
unmembered, unselved?

The body lays down its aggregate of cells,
joints its fine selvages. Someone is dead,
all bafflement and harm, yet someone else
will come to the end of a long darkness
as life rolls out its bright morsels.

The carousel of bags folds and unfolds its steel
leaves, carrying what we thought we needed.

Valerie Nieman

A Moment's Peace

Not that she's not the finest
woman a man could have,
you understand, as steady
as the chestnut beams
that hold up this house,
heart solid like good oak.
But for months I've been
waiting to slip away,
waiting on a time her heartbeat
and breath didn't fill all the house
and hold my life to my ribs.
A moment's peace
so that like a scarred old tomcat
I could slip away
and die without grief.

A miner's life goes on
as long as he feels
the shift of the earth around him,
knows the strain of slate
against roof bolts,
the dead air, the black damp
and the gas. I've felt my death
waiting for me before—once
I was buried to my waist
in a roof fall, one time
pinned against the face—
but death closed its red eyes and retreated
when the rescue teams came.

It's been here
waiting a long time, now,
in the useless hollows of my lungs:
black lung, they say, and emphysema,
the word like air hissing out
a punctured chest.
But Norma, this time,
shakes her fist in the face of death.
She stands over me
like a cat with one kitten,
like a slender pine tree
rooting together the broken face of a cliff.

I hear the mailman's pickup
grinding up the road;
he's a friend, unseen,
a friend like any man whose cap light
shines upon you in a close place,
promising relief.
The mailman doesn't realize
that the minute Norma takes to run down
and get the letters
is the day's freedom for me,
the only time she leaves
this house. Other people come and go,
she stays, her breaths drawing deep
and urging my own shallow
sucking at the bottled oxygen,
the labor of thirty dark years
waged all over again
in my tunneled lungs.
Norma and I, we are flesh of each other's flesh
and closer than ribs, even
the stacked bones of the spine.

She's back, pushing into the squeal
of the screen door,
shuffling the letters
and the printed circulars
that I read cover to cover,
prices compared, the soft colors
of women's sweaters that I never
before had the want or time to consider.
"Bills?" I ask,
the oxygen vibrating in my nostrils.
"Some. And there's a letter
here for Mr. Sam" – her nose wrinkles –
"Harry must've mixed the bundles."
"Oh," I say, but can't
summon the breath for more.

"It's government, got to be
important," she says. "And no mail
again 'til Tuesday."
I see her gauging the distance
to the old man's house,
five minutes at most.
"I suppose I ought to run it down to him."
She looks at me, propped
in the white of my hospital bed,
and I try not to whisper
go, go.
"I'll just be a minute,"
and she leans over and kisses my chin.

The screen door squalls
and bounces shut,
but she stands outside.
I can feel her, waiting, listening,
I breathe in and, struggling, out.

Her shoes crunch on the gravel,
down the driveway,
past the mailbox like a guarded gate
and onto the road.

I've been portioning out
my breaths, waiting.
The house is quiet, absolutely
quiet; it eases like a church
when the parishioners have gone
and the flowers have been taken
from the altar.
The window glass shivers,
feeling that she's gone, the linoleum
sighs with a strain relieved,
the water pipes sweat.
I see a bird's shadow move across
the window glass.
I see the shadows of the trees
on the floor
like the branches of a thicket,
green shade against the July sun,
a retreating place.
              I see my breath move across
the light, swirling
the bits of dust
and then they swim undisturbed.

Recovery From Death
of Family or Friends

One for
Father, one for
Mother. Two for my sweet brothers

—Cathy Smith Bowers

Cathy Smith Bowers

Peace Lilies

I collect them now, it seems. Like
sea-shells or old
thimbles. One for
Father. One for

Mother. Two for my sweet brothers.
Odd how little
they require of
me. Unlike the

ones they were sent in memory
of. No sudden
shrilling of the
phone. No harried

midnight flights. Only a little
water now and
then. Scant food and
light. See how I've

brought them all together here in
this shaded space
beyond the stairs.
Even when they

thirst, they summon me with nothing
more than a soft,
indifferent furl-
ing of their leaves.

Carolyn Kreiter-Foronda

Mother

I fear night
        until I find
                moon.
After dark, she scoops me
        up into her
                brightness
where I wander
        among spirits
                let loose
from the heavens: my mother,
        thirty years
                dead,
visits me often.
        Sometimes I see her
                running free
through luminous fields.
        Once from a cloud's
                savannah
she tamed a thunderbolt's
        whiplike snap
                at my feet.
Tonight moon dips
        into *Sagrada Familia*,
                Notre Dame,
into all of the world's churches.
        Mother alights in the sanctum
                of my heart.
Here, she teaches me
        about stone's durability,
                what it means

to outlast illness,
          how to take
                the years
I've been given and to fling
          them into air
                so they multiply,
so they ring through darkness.
          I gather up
                her words,
then retreat to my study.
          In the picture of us
                on the wall,
I am a child, kneeling
          at her feet,
                listening.

Susan Meyers

That Year
—for my mother

When the black-eyed susans begin to bloom
in the backyard, and the moonbeam coreopsis
bursts into tiny stars, I think of the year

I banished yellow from my life. It was the year
I dug up the lantana, when I didn't plant
narcissus and all the buttery bulbs

but chose white, and a little blue, for the garden
without knowing that I was readying
for two long years of her dying. The next spring

I painted our kitchen, once a lemony gloss, ecru.
I threw out from my closet all the blouses
hinting, from their hangers, of glad canaries.

Beginning that fall I dressed in a dull haze
of beige, toning myself down for the end.
I ignored the incandescence of morning, the amber

of dusk, and leaned to clouds billowed in black.
The week in November she died I loaded the trunk
of my car with flats of pansies, three sacks of bulbs.

I wanted my hands working the dirt, a dark loam
that would spring into jonquils, daffodils—bright
coronas of yellow, and yellow, and yellow.

Meir Wieseltier
    translated from Hebrew by *Shirley Kaufman*

Letter 2

Your mouth is filled with cotton wool according to their custom,
not satisfied with the dust we'll soon eat,
extractors of superfluous gold from the shamed mouth.
But they can't extract the panicky stare of the dead.
And I am the identifier, oh yes I identify: this is my mother
winter born, winter corpse, mother.

Even then your body betrayed you, that first winter
on the great trek east from the besieged city,
in out-of-the-way railroad stations, among all the other mothers
and children of DPs screaming on top of the bundles.
Even then it betrayed you, withheld its milk, and you
panicky like the dead with the load of your heavy infant
(his impossible weight almost finished you in your ninth month)
growing lighter every day, every day, every station of the flight.

The two of us survived many times in this life,
each of us alone, each in a separate flight.

If there were other worlds
our reunion wouldn't be that far off.
My hair already glints with steel like yours
and it's clear I look more and more like your father.
Oh there's so much we'll never get straight.
There are endless folds in the staring space of time.

In the shadow of run-down buildings, at odd hours
I'll recover the clues to your past with a skill
not much greater than yours reading my future,

but I won't complain or despair of your memory.
From now on we won't move away from each other, we'll come a little
       closer,

a thin and tentative closeness, and very one-sided.
But my hand in your illusory hand, I'll keep drawing near
to the beneficent ease of your smile flickering before my cerebral eye,
to the traces of truths you stored in disordered drawers
under crumpled letters, photographs, hairpins,
bunches of old jewelry, new medicine,
dried flowers from withered gardens:

the stuff of our lives is the gold of transience
poured down our warm throats thirsting for milk.

Satyendra Srivastava

The Most Satisfying Moment

It was the last glance
Of an immortal look
The touch of a dying
Gentle spark
The echo of a bursting glacier within
A silent cry
From a dried hollow throat
It was my mother's last thirst
The word *pani* only half uttered
I gently poured water from a spoon
She gulped a few drops
And tried to look again
Perhaps to bless me
Perhaps to tell me
How the last drip of life's nectar tasted
But she couldn't
A gasp
The water dropped back on her
Parched wounded lips
And she was gone
And I felt elevated
As never before
Quenching the last thirst
Is the most satisfying moment

Joseph Enzweiler

The Immense

We stand in the room at ten o'clock
these minutes after his death,
the blue tube removed, the machine
that breathed beside him, gone.
His last breath like a pendulum
is caught and held. How thin
his legs are beneath the sheet,
the first night of his journey
and of ours, left behind.

We look down together, we look
alone, his three boys, each man
a kind of architecture with its
struts of pain and wonder.
The water glass is silent forever
beside the swivel table. Those cigarettes
seem almost light now, free
of their fate. The night stand,
a Guy Lombardo tape, that little box
of photographs he kept for years
snap their tethers and float away.
The room is large, so large now.

Tomorrow or the next the three of us
will lock together, make a single
dwelling to carry him in.
I'll feel his pin-striped suit,
touch the fingers hard as ceramic,
straighten his tie.

Through cross traffic down bright
September roads, we'll merge
in the work day and follow him
to Mass, locked down in some black
Cadillac, toward our consolation
and his ground.

But now, the night is here, passing
over the ceiling tiles, in the poured
darkness of his mouth. Outside
the neighborhood moves on;
its quiet houses breathe. But tonight
I cannot walk away as I once did.
I'm in these older clothes.

Beside the bed our shoulders
nearly touch in lamp light that is
brittle and immense. We are
three angels suddenly given bones.
The floor reaches into us.

But days when I was ten, how the wind
cut through the houses, the great
hollow subdivisions of those years.
In a wool coat, with a ladder
and steel drill in the dim morning hours,
each room whistled the Missouri waltz.

I felt so side by side with him,
it showed in my hands and stride.
I'd make a fire from scraps of lumber,
then my first cup of coffee
on the running board, cream
and sugar and the truck in mud.

Some days I nearly cried to leave
a house to its barren windy corners.
Not for themselves, but for the spaces
in between where work was done,
the wall-less, roofless places.

Who bears the brunt of love?
All the factories and the sun,
not us alone, orderlies who hurry past
with eyes like shale, a pregnant nurse
on the phone in troubled whispers,
and all who rise tomorrow
and climb back on the wondrous machine,
though for them it's only a day,
only the night shift.

Rose says to us, "You can touch him
if you want." When I am there
alone, I do, along one arm,
across his folded hands,
those frail enormities,
goodbye and thanks, those days
were cold and good.

Look hard one time
at the man he had been.
When I turn and let him go,
I am a little boy again.

Jane Gentry

In the Moment of My Death:
For My Father

You were simple, I suppose,
delighted by life
so that sickness and death
came to you as a surprise
out of the shadows of your heart.

In the moment of my death
may your old happiness light my way,
and the image of your face
smiling, happy at my coming,
be a lantern in the dark.

Rachel Eliza Griffiths

Portrait: Waking as a Girl
—for my father

Even then I recognized the drift, even then, as I awoke
during those years, to girlhood. Beyond words,
I named the blizzard of senses that overwhelmed
language. From dreams to the silent gray
of winter, I did not speak.

Waking depended on the myrrh of his aftershave
to guide my eyes into focus: my father
in a charcoal suit, his gold wedding band
wet from the single splash of water
that rinsed his face, after he used Listerine.

From the nocturne ghosts to the geography
of a pillow, the scent arrived to wake me.
Between the wood bureau and the creaking radiators,
I stumbled to the bathroom's tunnel of light.

And when I could not (having become
a woman) understand much of my father's life,
I relied on the old musk that clung to the collars
of my father's suits – the closets that I opened to become
his girl again when no one thought
I cared anymore.

How I chased the silent essence of his sacrifices
in my miserable independence.
How, even now, my dark head mourns him
on its pillow in an empty room.

Gail Peck

I'll Never

smell lilies again
without thinking of those
brought to me after my sister's death.
This time I chose them,
wide petals yawning over the vase.
I go outside to look for her
in the eyes of the cardinal.
Snow flurries no one predicted—
perhaps these are the ashes
of the dead, now pure.
I open my mouth and let them settle.

Martha Collins

The Orange Room

—*for Mary Anne Heyward Ferguson*
and Alfred Riggs Ferguson (1915-1974)

Today is Pentecost, in the calendar of my mind,
where pages turn and turn, back and back,
and back again. I turn to them
who took me in, the year I married darkness.

Going out for oranges again,
though that was a far country, another sea.
For the first time, my hand on the tree.
Sun in the bowl of the hills.

I married oranges. Eggs and juice.
I ate my words, painted that country.
I burned my words in a coffee can.
I did it again, but not again.

Then I ate the blackened fruit.
Fire burns to the core, I said.
There's nothing to be said, in final lines.

At the end of a long hall, his arms.
I bore no gifts. They fed my need.
A room, orange, with dark wood walls.
Three windows, door. Sun, over the sea.

I loved them, man-and-woman,
as man loves woman, woman man.
They loved me, woman-daughter.
No one knew the hour. They gave me time.

Two orange beds in the orange room.
Brandy at midnight. They evened my sleep.
When I woke, not knowing who I was,
they eased me into morning. He made coffee.

It is a simple fact: he died.
But I swear, as I sat in the graveyard grass,
a hint of mist, and that was all.
It licks my mind like fire.

Today is her birthday, in the calendar of the world.
My sister, who was my mother.
I have grown. They helped me grow.
A green green tree with bright orange fruit.

I loved a man, when he brought me coffee.
He gave me this black pen, this gold tongue.
Bless him, too, in love's orange fire.
Give him vision, time, in these late days.

One more turn, before the last:

Where the gold tongue forks, the black fire,
cleaving apart and unto, in a word.
This is the pen my hand must hold,
this forked and unforked tongue.

Bless them at last. Thanks to the end.
I have remembered where I am going.
Without a partner, dust will dance.
His ashes will not burn. His silence sings.

Jennifer Barber

Hymns in the Wind

—in mem. A. F.

1
All day the rain
wanted to fall.

All night, all fall
I wanted a name
for what I was
without.

Now I know
night enters me,

its sadness
a sailing ship
in the light
beneath each star.

2
A candle, a match,
the window going blind.

Snails on the cabbages
wait for the rain

sowing only itself,
drowning the magpies' cries,

black and white
wings through a tree.

3
I've imagined you
standing in the square

of an old city.
The shops are closed.

No bustle, no cars.
Language,

yours alone,
drifts on the still air.

4
Dust lifts
through my room,
          touching down
too lightly to be swept.

A flock of birds
          swerves above
the shed,

a sudden whole
in the confusion of its pieces.

5
I lit the kindling:
a forest in the grate
woke inside
an orange city.

Can you hear
this place
in a place
I made for you?

6

Stray bees, returning,
bend the wildflowers.

All night the rigging
of the wind

throws me rope
ladders, and lets go.

7

North of the highway,
empty trees.

The wind I probe
for absences

is only a path
for rain,

the weight of distance
bearing down.

Ilya Kaminsky

Author's Prayer

If I speak for the dead, I must leave
this animal of my body,

I must write the same poem over and over,
for an empty page is the white flag of their surrender.

If I speak for them, I must walk on the edge
of myself, I must live as a blind man

who runs through rooms without
touching the furniture.

Yes, I live. I can cross the streets asking "What year is it?"
I can dance in my sleep and laugh

in front of the mirror.
Even sleep is a prayer, Lord,

I will praise your madness, and
in a language not mine, speak

of music that wakes us, music
in which we move. For whatever I say

is a kind of petition, and the darkest
days must I praise.

Major Jackson

Allegheny

1.

What privilege I flaunt discarding time
   Like a swatch of faded, blue-jean sky
Addressing you as though the poem a clothesline
   & we, two cups that connect, speaking high
   Above the city—or is it more like I
Slow earth's spinning with my finger?
My pen a needle where the song lingers.

2.

Not out for the epic, I want a vault
   For my verbal wealth. I want a form
For my lyrical stealth. I want a malt
   To toast the public's health. I want a storm
   On my perfect shelf. I mourned
Your loss on the phone with Marie Howe.
You were her first love. I said, "How

3.

Would she want us to remember her?"
   She said, "As we do—in verse."
Then, "Do you think she'll reply to a letter?"
   She said, "The dead are terse."
   I got it, then I said, "Hearses
Should speed to graves in processions.
The living outnumber their phantoms."

4.

"Lady Paul Laurence Dunbar" is how
    I would have dispatched in your youth,—
Mother Keziah, assured you'd plough
    Words for dialectical truths,
    Named you thus. An insatiable sweet tooth
You had early for concentrated rhymes,
Flavorful as raspberry, orange, or lime.

5.

Possibly I want a hero, too. Tis
    Dry, true—those documentaries come
February striving for racial bliss.
    I would rather have sung "We Shall Overcome"
    At a Super Bowl than one more mind-numb
-Ing black-and-white clip of the unnamed hosed
In prayer. I would rather whole episodes

6.

Featuring year-round *Biography*'s:
    Black poets, surgeons, priests.
How more acrobatic do our teeth need to be?
    How many more laughs can a feast
    Of eyes, hard boiled, bulging, the leitmotif
Of the downtrodden graphic terror,
Sustain the birth of a nation? The nearer

7.

The prize, when some standup out-bugs
    His eyes. Law-upholding laughter
Follows like a stutter step as the Strug
    -Gle giggles, and a world of sufferers

Side-splits away their tears. That's why *Nigger*
No longer sticks like cotton in the throat.
Some black comics are the worst turncoats.

    8.

Many dance to forget. I knew a giant
  Who rolled down Broad blasting Led
Zeppelin in a ride. His gentle spirit
   Streamed along till his pain cracked & bled
   & left two brackish hawsers. He shed
What ached by shuttling open-aired, a means
I'd likely never forget, the scream

    9.

Of art, blood music caught in the strum
  Uncoiling from bedsprings. It's there
At our begetting, hurt that becomes
   A singular song. We add to the blare
   & din. We give it a window by a chair
& listen, nodding heads, rubbing chins,
& throw our hands up as if greeting friends.

    10.

I, myself, emerged from a dark cave lured
  By history and two visions. A romantic,
I stood in my b-boy stance, arms ruled,
   Angled back, head posed for the authentic—
   Up joined the Dark Room Collective.
Were I in Kentucky I would, even then,
Have united with the Affrilachians,

11.

So strong the urge to place my pen aside
   My generation. Ellis was our Pound.
We, the inheritors of your black pride,
   & he, loudest inkslinger with Strange, found
   A cadre to unselfconsciously sound
Off Hayden, Baraka, Dove, and Wright,
To become our next black literary lights.

12.

Light does not exist in a coffin,
   Both merely signifiers asserts Derrida.
I'm off for a cup of Starbucks coffee,
   & a lifespan sipped on DVD.
   Avoid the headlines by the jelly
Beans. How queasy war next to tins of mints.
Have you bought Musicology *by Prince?*

13.

Who did we not celebrate? America could
   Never deal with a diverse canon of poets.
I mean what it really means, and not just a cold
   Few hiding out in "Separate but equal"
   Magazines, really face a people's poetry.
This was the aim of the DRC,
to test the puddles of white supremacy.

Allison Hedge Coke
translated from Lakota by the author

Remembrance (*Wokiksuye*)

—*for Cangleska Maza*

Like a horse's tail
so thick, black
down past his waist
beautiful.   Look at this.
Chemotherapy—
white man's
man-made cancer . . .
doesn't distinguish
between good or bad
cells . . . just kills.
The spirit is connected
to the hair at the
crown center   spirit lock.
The hair falls,
the spirit goes,
the will is
connected no more.
Leukemia—
cancer of the
White
Blood Cell.
Man of the allies
Man of the ones who scatter
The Red Nations   hold good life wellness, no
Sickness, pitiful
a Holy Road I am walking
a ghost I am walking with
crying in mourning
crying

I will remember you
will remember, memorialize
I most sincerely thank you
remember me
I walk a Red Road
I walk a Good Road
With courage I now take
I am happy, I am happy
Again—today
today is a good day
I knew him well.

Steven Cramer

Everyone Who Left Us

Everyone who left us we find everywhere.
It's easier, now, to look them in the eyes—
At gravesites, in bed, when the phone rings.
Of course, we wonder if they think of us.

It's easier, now, to look them in the eyes,
Imagine touching a hand, listening to them talk.
Of course, we wonder if they think of us
When nights, like tonight, turn salty, warm.

Imagine touching a hand, listening to them talk—
Hard to believe they're capable of such coldness.
When nights, like tonight, turn salty, warm,
We think of calling them, leaving messages.

Hard to believe they're capable of such coldness—
No color, no pulse, not even a nerve reaction.
We think of calling them, leaving messages
Vivid with news we're sure they'd want to know.

No color, no pulse, not even a nerve reaction:
We close our eyes in order not to see them.
Vivid with news we're sure they'd want to know
We don't blame them, really. They weren't cruel.

We close our eyes in order not to see them
Reading, making love, or falling asleep.
We don't blame them, really. They weren't cruel,
Though it hurts every time we think of them:

Reading, making love, or falling asleep,
Enjoying the usual pleasures and boredoms.
Though it hurts every time we think of them,
Like a taste we can't swallow their names stay.

Enjoying the usual pleasures and boredoms,
Then, they leave us the look of their faces
Like a taste we can't swallow. Their names stay,
Diminishing our own, getting in the way

At gravesites, in bed, when the phone rings.
Everyone who left us we find everywhere,
Then they leave us, the look of their faces
Diminishing, our own getting in the way.

Linda Annas Ferguson

What Would Jesus Say

if I asked him about the dream
I had last night of people falling
through my bedroom ceiling?

Would he explain in parables and metaphors
how the soft losses of the heart
break through the thick rind of the mind

or would he say nothing, only show me
clouds that form puzzles in the sky,
make thunder rumble in the distance,
his words sighing their meaning?

The dirt we were has nothing to tell us
as we bury our dead,
make tombstones that read:
Here lie music, art, and poetry.

Gardeners come to cut weeds
that tumble with gravity.
On our way back to sleeping and waking
we step on cracks in the sidewalk

that could be a warning
we might be falling toward God.

Recovery From Stresses of Living

I collapsed, exhausted, on my side of the unmade bed

—Simon Armitage

Rita Dove

Fox Trot Fridays

Thank the stars there's a day
each week to tuck in

the grief, lift your pearls, and
stride brush stride

quick-quick with a
heel-ball-toe. Smooth

as Nat King Cole's
slow satin smile,

easy as taking
one day at a time:

one man and
one woman,

rib to rib,
with no heartbreak in sight—

just the sweep of Paradise
and the space of a song

to count all the wonders in it.

Kevin Simmonds

After Katrina

There's no Sabbath in this house.
Just work.

The black of garbage bags,
yellow-cinched throats opening
to gloved hands.

Black tombs along the road now,
proof she knew to cherish
the passing things,

even those muted before the water came
before the mold's grotesquerie
and the wooden house choked on bones.

My aunt wades through the wreckage, failing
no matter how hard she tries
at letting go.

I look on glad at her failing,
her slow rites
fingering what she'd once been given to care for.

The waistbands of her husband's briefs
elastic as memory;
the blank stare of rotted drawers,

their irises of folded linen still,
smelling of soap and wood
and clean hands.

Daylight through the silent windows
and I'm sure now: Today is Sabbath,
the work we do, prayer.

I know what she releases into the garbage bags,
shiny like wet skins of seals
beached on the shore of this house.

Gail Rudd Entrekin

Wailing

I hiked down the steep rocky path
to the river, where someone
had impossibly hauled wood
for a small house, or shack really,
now deserted, and I climbed
over boulders in the sand,
finally reached the water
high and rushing in spring flood,
shinnied up and sat
on a smooth edge in the sun.
My German shepherd scrabbled below me,
lying down in the cold current,
lapping loudly and then subsiding
so the river was the only sound,
miles from anywhere, peace. And then
a loud unexpected noise,
a sob breaking out
into the open, another, the dog and I—
eyes meeting in mutual surprise—
What does it mean?
And then for a long time there was crying,
a wailing, the river accepting it all,
the whole weight of it
breaking up, shifting, lifting
out of my chest and returning
on the wind.

And when it was quiet again,
I climbed down onto the sand,
found a round stone for my pocket,
planted a tall tapered rock
pointing upward
standing
for my intention.

Simon Armitage

Hercules

After not taking the cat to the vet's for a jab,
not putting the garden hose back in the garden shed,
not tracking something down, not bringing bacon home,
not blacking the kitchen stove with black lead,

after not finding the dead bird the cat smuggled in,
not not talking bullshit on the phone all day to friends,
not paying the blacksmith cash instead of a cheque,
not bringing the washing into the house when it rained,

after not having the spine to dig the vegetable patch,
not picking the fruit before the fruit went bad,
after not walking the dog once all day for crying out loud
I collapsed, exhausted, on my side of the unmade bed.

Ed Madden

Weekend

The hammock frame has cracked in the rain—
keel of wet wood, an unbuilt boat—
still good you say, just needs some glue
and a clamp, but it's too damp to do it

right now, a project for another day.
In the wet grass, some broken glass—
and a gash on your left foot, the heel.
You limp to the steps and inside to the tub,

wash the red slash and dab it with salve,
tamp down the bandage tabs
on wet skin—they'll hold. The day
is damp and cold. We'll go to Lowe's

later. The hammock is furled in the shed.
A dream of leisure dangles in the frame.

Rebecca McClanahan

There Are Days

There are days when nothing
especially goes right but nothing
wrong, and you find yourself
writing to your sister-in-law
to thank her for the lemon cake
she baked that time, and for loving
your brother all these years.
Three, maybe four times that day
you praise whoever is responsible
for letting you pee so easily,
without pain, without the tubes
and bags your uncle rolled on a cart
beside him that last year. You dig
in the garden until sweat pearls
your lip and you taste the salt
you have made, remembering the poem
a small girl wrote after her father was shot:
I love myself because I am not dead.
In bed that night you spread your toes.
The furnace of your brain warms
the pillow, the heart's engine ticks,
and the lungs, those meaty wings,
flutter and empty, flutter
and empty, lifting you into sleep.

Nancy Tupper Ling

Another New England Winter

By February we're weary.
Four o'clock's darkness
descends again over
our sterile snow drifts,
trapping us behind doors,
drawn curtains that keep
drafts and neighbors at bay.
Even diehard Yankees wonder
if spring will come.

We've faced such dormancy
before: five years waiting
for a tiny life to flower
inside my womb. Then, too,
we shut shades early
against sounds, voices
of nearby children
sledding into our gully,
alone with Mourning.

Come March we notice
first buds unfurling.
We crack our windows,
let in light breezes.
They carry pollen,
fresh and sticky
to our sills.

Carole Baldock

Now That May Is Here

Preston of all places
for the first long distance train journey
once back home. Memory stabs
with all its echoes,
mellowing only
with the dwindling sun
when the skies catch fire. Dowsed
as night is snatched up, then overflowing
all the green, green world,
houses, roads, towns, reduced to grey.

I remember
we hoped to spot Mount Fuji.
How clear, how near it seemed
though the speed of the *Shinkansen*
repeatedly blotted it out,
bisected it with telegraph poles.
A photo demanded the skills
of an Arcade addict.
Yes, now I remember,
same sun, same skies.

Deema Shehabi

At the Dome of the Rock

Jerusalem in the afternoon is the bitterness of two hundred
winter-bare olive trees fallen in the distance. Jerusalem
in the soft afternoon is a woman sitting at the edge of the Mosque
with her dried-up knees tucked beneath her, listening to shipwrecks
of holy words. If you sit beside her under the stone arch facing the Old City,
beneath the lacquered air that hooks into every crevice of skin,
your blood will unleash with her dreams, the Dome
will undulate gold, and her exhausted scars
will gleam across her overly kissed forehead.
She will ask you to come closer, and when you do,
she will lift the sea of her arms from the furls
of her chest and say: *this is the dim sky I have loved ever since I was a child.*

Kate Gale

Sex After Babies

I haven't written a sex poem
for months I've had a baby
then another these two babies
take the place of sex for me
my husband cannot see the connection
between babies and sex
he says babies and sex
are two different matters
he wants to straighten out
any mixup on that
I have to explain
the babies have taken
the part of me
that wants sex
they went barreling through
took that part with them
he wants to know what part
and when will it come back
I say I don't know later
maybe tomorrow
he frowns which reminds me
of something I heard
give it to them at home
or they'll come home with the clap
I say, dear it's come back
and he says, it's here, now?
so delighted, so like the boy I married
that I am ready to play
I have it for a while
hoping that whatever
it is
will come back.

Jeffrey Levine

Thé Dansant

See her down there? Our planet as a child—
red, eruptive, difficult, Jurassic, lost.
At Olduvai Gorge, a flat-headed chunk of skull gathers
in the fetid air, one millennium into another.

Near Lake Turkana, the twelve-year-old who went for water
two million years ago—whose narrow brow still lards the plain.
Jaw fragments, leg and hand bones. A scattering
of hackberry seeds. Teeth. Those, too.
It got cold, then colder. You see?

One night the moon diminished, next the sun.
Still, we forgive the lightning, promise children light follows night.
What do we know? It pleases us to think it might.
Let it be so, as it pleased the kids to dream *thele*,
dream *thelyblast*, dream the lee wash of night itself.

Only an epoch pause, each of us
a furrowed, hair-matted thing,
staring at the ice-borne rim just long enough
to scatter seeds across the melt.

Bernardo Atxaga

Death and the Zebras

We were 157 zebras
galloping across the parched plain,
I ran behind zebra 24,
25 and 26,
ahead of 61 and 62
and suddenly we were overtaken with a jump
by 118 and 119,
both of them shouting *river, river*,
and 25, very happy, repeated *river, river*,
and suddenly 130 reached us
running, shouting, very happy, *river, river*,
and 25 took a left turn
ahead of 24 and 26
and suddenly I saw the sun on the river
sparkling full sparkly splashes
and 8 and 9 passed me
running in the opposite direction
with their mouths full of water
and wet legs and wet chests
very happy, shouting *go, go, go*
and I suddenly collided with 5 and 7
who were also running in the opposite direction
but shouting *crocodiles, crocodiles*,
and then 6 and 30 and 14 ran past us
very frightened, shouting, *crocodiles, crocodiles, go, go, go*
and I drank water, I drank sparkling water
full of sparkly splashes and sun
crocodile, crocodile, shouted 25, very frightened,
crocodile, I repeated, rearing back;

and running very frightened in the opposite direction
I suddenly collided with 149
and 150 and 151,
running, shouting, very happy, *river*, *river*,
crocodiles, *crocodiles*, I shouted back, very frightened
with my mouth full of water
and wet legs and wet chest.
I kept galloping across the parched plain
behind 24 and 26
ahead of 60 and 61
and suddenly I saw, suddenly I saw a gap
between 24 and 26, a gap
and I kept galloping across the parched plain
and I saw the gap again, the gap again,
between 24 and 26
and suddenly I jumped and filled the gap.

We were 149 zebras
galloping across the parched plain,
and ahead of me were 12, 13
and 14, and behind me were
43 and 44.

In Appreciation

This anthology began with Fred Marchant. The Poetry of Recovery was conceived in the week following a lunch with Fred during the Associated Writing Programs Conference in Atlanta (2007) when he knocked me into silence with these words: "Why don't you become a poetry publisher?"

Fred had just heard my very discouraging answer to his previous question: "How's your manuscript going?" He listened silently to my tale of a thousand rejections, and then kicked me down this path. Thank you, Fred. Whatever success this book has reflects back to that moment.

The Poetry of Recovery was born.

A call for submissions went out via Cave Canem, CRWOPPS, Wom-Po, and other listservs along with a few targeted advertisements in literary journals. I owe specific thanks to Susan Meyers, who spread the word through her vast network.

The Poetry of Recovery had begun to crawl.

An Iranian poet, Farideh Hassanzadeh, answered my call with deeply moving poems from Tehran and spread the word and I began to receive poems from India, Turkey, Bosnia, which became the root of this anthology's international perspective.

The Poetry of Recovery took its first steps.

Then, one day I received an email out of the blue from Annie Finch: "Farideh Hassanzadeh said that I should send you some poems," with an attachment of 7 poems. Later in the same week in April 2007, I received a submission from Martha Collins in reply to my cold-call email. Thanks, Farideh. Thanks, Annie. Thanks, Martha.

The Poetry of Recovery began its run to your hands.

The number of hands holding this anthology is due in large part to the expertise of Marjory Wentworth who directed my efforts to make you aware of this book.

Deepest appreciation to Cathy Smith Bowers for her guidance and editing on this project and others over many years. To Rebecca McClanahan, Ron Rash, Alan Michael Parker, Major Jackson, and Steven Cramer—thanks for attaching my right brain to my left-brained pen and for your contributions to this anthology. To Ellis Rubinstein, Frank Finn, and William S. Rukeyser, early editorial mentors, everlasting gratitude for a foundation well built.

Special thanks to Afaa Michael Weaver and Nicholas Mazza for believing in this project enough to write forewords.

Grateful and bountiful thanks to more than I can name among therapists and clergy: Dr. Mazza, editor of the *Journal of Poetry Therapy*; Lauren Keller of the National Association of Poetry Therapy; Rev. Lindsey Armstrong; and theologians Mark Douglas, Ph.D., and Walter Brueggemann, Ph.D. Your support and encouragement of The Poetry of Recovery confirmed that I was on the right path.

To Kevin Watson, publisher at Press 53, deepest gratitude for sharing his expertise and knowledge and for his hands-on work on the design, production, and printing of this anthology.

To Mary L. Akers, co-author of *Radical Gratitude and Other Life Lessons Learned in Siberia*, for her counsel on this anthology's structure and format, my radical gratitude.

Finally, thanks to the hundreds of poets who submitted their work. I enjoyed the reading. I wish I could have used more. And to all poets laboring at their desks, writing poems of recovery—Keep at it! I look forward to reading your work in the future.

Tom Lombardo
Editor
After Shocks: The Poetry of Recovery for Life-Shattering Events

Notes on the Poems

Birthday Present by Tom Lombardo page 51
Namesti Square is in Prague, Czech Republic.

(*what has anchored us*) by Rachel Tzvia Back page 69
Sakhnin is a town in Galilee, at the center of riots by Israeli Arabs in October 2000. The riots left 13 Israeli citizens dead, 12 of whom were Israeli Arabs. The riots were part of the beginning of the Al-Aksa Intifadah—the second Intifadah—sparked by Ariel Sharon's visit to the Dome of the Rock/Temple Mount area.

2000 lbs. by Brian Turner page 73
Inshallah is Arabic for "if Allah wills" or "God willing." *Habib* is Arabic for "beloved."

The Wall by Nazand Begikhani page 80
Halabja is the town in the Kurdish region of Northern Iraq that was the site of a chemical attack by the regime of Saddam Hussein on Iraqi Kurds on March 16, 1988, which killed 5,000 civilians, 75 percent of them women and children.

Sir Winston Churchill Knew My Mother by Satyendra Srivastava page 87
Mussoorie is located in the Garhwal hills in the Indian state of Uttarakhand in the foothills of the Himalaya ranges. "That crazy naked fakir" is, of course, Mohandas K. Ghandi, who led the peaceful revolution of resistance that gained India's independence from Great Britain in 1947.

To the Children of Prison and Exile by Majid Naficy page 95
The literal meanings of the Farsi names Cheshmeh, Roza, and Sulmaz are "spring," "rose," and "everlasting," respectively.

Ah, Los Angeles by Majid Naficy page 99
The Parsees are the descendants of Zoroastrians who emigrated from Iran to Gujarat, India during the Arab conquests. In 1599, Bahman Key Qobâd, a Gujarati Parsee, wrote an epic poem in which he depicts such a migration on a ship from the Straits of Hormoz in the Persian Gulf to the port of Sanjan in India. The *sadra* and *kusti* are special tunics and belts worn by Zoroastrians after puberty.

A Brief Informal History by J. P. Dancing Bear page 101
Jim Thorpe, born in 1888 of mixed Native American and white ancestry, was raised in the Sac and Fox Nation. Thorpe won Olympic gold medals in the pentathlon and decathlon in 1912, played American football at Carlisle College and professionally. He was stripped of his Olympic titles for playing minor league baseball for pay before competing in the Olympics. Thorpe was named the greatest athlete of the first half of the 20th Century by the Associated Press in 1950, and ranked third on the AP list of athletes of the century in 1999. After his professional sports career ended, Thorpe lived in abject poverty. In 1983, thirty years after his death, his Olympic medals were restored.

Equilibrium by Margaret Chula page 102
Ikebana is the traditional Japanese art of arranging flowers. *Issei*, a Japanese word meaning literally "first generation," is a term used in North and South America to refer to Japanese who emigrated to those continents in the years preceding World War II. Shortly after the entry of the United States into World War II, Japanese Americans, roughly 110,000 men, women, and children, including those born in the U.S., were relocated to internment camps in desert areas of Arizona, California, Utah, Idaho, Colorado, and Wyoming, where they spent the entire war living under conditions akin to prisoners of war. The last of the camps was closed in March 1946. In 1988, legislation apologized for the internment on behalf of the U.S. government, and beginning in 1990, the U.S. government paid reparations to surviving internees.

Breathing Forward in America by Lisha Adela Garcia page 104
Mijares is a ballad-pop singer who took the Latin music world by storm
after his album debut in 1985.

Last Service by Ron Rash page 105
In the early 1970s, despite fervent opposition by the inhabitants of Jocassee
Valley, South Carolina, Duke Power Company built a dam to create the
Jocassee Reservoir. Both the living and the dead were evicted from the
valley. Hundreds of graves were dug up and their contents reburied in
cemeteries outside the valley. The living continued to visit their churches,
by boat as the waters rose, until the churches were inundated. The
reservoir reached full capacity in 1974. In the Cherokee language, *Jocassee*
means "place of the lost."

The Resolve by Satyendra Srivastava page 148
Paki is derogatory slang used in the U.K. to refer to immigrants from
Pakistan. In its broader slang usage, it refers pejoratively to any non-
white immigrant.

For the Confederate Dead by Kevin Young page 151
Line 23, "heighth" [sic]. Line 52, "seed" [sic].

From Farewell to Recsk by György Faludy page 161
Forced labor camps in Hungary were closed in 1953 after Soviet dictator
Stalin's death. The translation herein comprises fragments from the longer
poem. Zsuzsa was Faludy's young wife who waited for him without any
news or communication.

Salvage Anthropology by Bette Lynch Husted page 163
Franz Boas is considered both the founder of modern anthropology as
well as the father of American anthropology. Boas gave modern
anthropology its rigorous scientific methodology, patterned after the
natural sciences. Boas originated the notion of culture as learned behavior,
going against the cultural evolutionary theory prevalent at the time that
labeled Native Americans, Africans, etc., as primitive or inferior peoples,

not as evolved as the superior Europeans. As a teacher, principally at Columbia University, he served as mentor to many of the top names in American anthropology, including Alfred Kroeber and Margaret Mead. Franz Boas was born in Minden, Germany on July 9, 1858.

This New Never by J. Stephen Rhodes page 170
The Little Flower of Lisieux is the Roman Catholic Saint Thérèse de Lisieux (1873–1897), who entered the Carmelite order of nuns at the age of 15. She is known for her "Little Way." In her quest for sanctity, she believed that it was not necessary to accomplish heroic acts in order to attain holiness and to express her love of God. She wrote, "The only way I can prove my love is by scattering flowers and these flowers are every little sacrifice, every glance and word, and the doing of the least actions for love." St. Thérèse's spiritual memoir, *L'histoire d'une âme* ("The Story of a Soul") was published posthumously and became the religious best-seller of the 20th century.

(*their sons my sons*) by Rachel Tzvia Back page 182
In Gaza, Jan. 2005, an Israeli bomb was dropped on 12 boys in a strawberry field. Seven boys were killed; the five survivors all lost limbs.

Missive From Shakaland by Liesl Jobson page 209
The term *Sangoma* is used to describe a holy man or woman within the tradition of the Zulu, Swazi, Xhosa and Ndebele native peoples of Southern Africa. A sangoma is a practitioner of herbal medicine, divination, and counseling. The sangoma play a crucial part of tribal life and customs in everyday affairs as mediators, often preventing internal arguments, healing the wounded souls, motivating recovery throughout the community.

Ikebana by Genie Cotner page 238
Ikebana is the traditional Japanese art of arranging flowers.

Praying for Miracles at Velankani Amman's Shrine, Tamil Nadu by Pramila Venkateswaran page 251

Velankani is the location in Tamil Nadu of a shrine to the Blessed Virgin Mary, a Roman Catholic icon. The local people refer to the Virgin as Velankani Amman. *Amman* is the Hindi term for Goddess Mother. People of many faiths in the region believe Velankani Amman to be miraculous.

Mother by Carolyn Kreiter-Foronda page 260
Temple de la Sagrada Familia is an unfinished church designed by Antoni Gaudi in Barcelona, Spain.

Letter 2 by Meir Wieseltier page 263
DPs were Displaced Persons. At the end of World War II, hundreds of thousands of civilians were refugees—called at the time Displaced Persons—of battles, prisons, and concentration camps. Relocation camps were set up by the Allies and nonprofit groups for DPs until those refugees could find a place to go, either back to their homes or to other countries. Mr. Wieseltier's family relocated to Israel.

The Most Satisfying Moment by Satyendra Srivastava page 265
Pani is Hindi for water.

Allegheny by Major Jackson page 281
DRC is the Dark Room Collective. The Dark Room Collective was founded in Boston in 1988 by a group of African American poets led by Thomas Sayers Ellis and Sharan Strange. The mission of the DRC was to form a community of established and emerging African American writers. Major Jackson, Natasha Trethewey, and Kevin Young were members of this group. This poem is drawn from a longer work entitled "Letter to Brooks," which begins with the salutation, "Dear Gwendolyn."

Now That May Is Here by Carole Baldock page 298
The *Shinkansen* is a network of high-speed railway lines in Japan. *Shinkansen* literally means "New Trunk Line," referring to the tracks, but the name is widely used in and outside Japan to refer to the trains running on the lines as well as the system as a whole.

Acknowledgments

Anthony S. Abbott's poem "The Man Who Speaks to His Daughter on Her 40th Birthday" from *The Man Who* (Main Street Rag 2007). Copyright © 2007 by Anthony S. Abbott. Reprinted by permission of the author.

Doug Anderson's poems "Outliving Our Ghosts" and "Recovery" from *The Moon Reflected Fire* (Alice James Books 1994). Copyright © 1994 by Doug Anderson. Reprinted with the permission of Alice James Books, Farmington, Maine.

Simon Armitage's poems "Poem" and "Hercules" from *Selected Poems* (Faber & Faber 2001). Copyright © 2001 by Simon Armitage. Reprinted with the permission of the author and Davis Goodwin Associates, Ltd., London.

Bernardo Atxaga's poem "Death and the Zebras" reprinted with permission of the author and Arc Publications, Todmorden, England. The poem recently appeared in English in *Six Basque Poets* (Arc Publications 2007) edited by the Basque author, editor, and critic Mari Jose Olaziregi.

Rachel Tzvia Back's poems "*(what has anchored us)*" and "*(their sons my sons)*" and "[When we no longer care]" from *On Ruins and Return* (Shearsman Books 2007). Copyright 2007 © by Rachel Tzvia Back. Reprinted with the permission of Shearsman Books, Ltd., London.

Mary Jo Bang's poem "You Were You Are Elegy" from *Elegy* (Graywolf Press 2007). Copyright 2007 © Mary Joe Bang. Reprinted with the permission of Graywolf Press, Saint Paul, Minnesota.

Jennifer Barber's poem "Hymns in the Wind" from *Rigging the Wind* (Kore Press 2003). Copyright © 2003 by Jennifer Barber. Reprinted with the permission of Kore Press, Tucson, Arizona, and the author.

Nazand Begikhani's poems "Illusion" and "The Wall" and "Exile" from *Bells of Speech* (Ambit Books 2006). Copyright © 2006 by Nazand Begikhani. Reprinted with the permission of Ambit Books, London.

Pam Bernard's poem "September 13" from *My Own Hundred Doors* (Bright Hill Press 1996). Copyright © 1996 by Pam Bernard. Reprinted with the permission of the author. Her poem "[As the landscape turns melancholic]" from her forthcoming manuscript *Blood Garden: an elegy for Raymond* (WordTech Editions), a poetic narrative of her father's experiences as an infantryman in World War I, first appeared in *Main Street Rag*. Reprinted with the permission of the author. The epigraph in "September 13" is excerpted from "Sestina" by Elizabeth Bishop (collected in *Elizabeth Bishop: the Collected Poems* Farrar Strauss & Giroux 1974).

Sonja Besford's poem "subjects in the cold winter of '93/'94 belgrade" from *memories of summers in brist near gradac and other poems* (Ambit Books 2006). Copyright © 2006 by Sonja Besford. Reprinted with the permission of Ambit Books, London.

Laurel Blossom's poem "The Intemperate Zone" from *Degrees of Latitude* (Four Way Books 2007). Copyright © 2007 by Laurel Blossom. Reprinted with the permission of Four Way Books, New York.

David Bottoms' poems "In a U-Haul North of Damascus" and "A Daughter's Fever" from *Armored Hearts: Selected and New Poems* (Copper Canyon Press 1994). Copyright © 1994 by David Bottoms. Reprinted with the permission of Copper Canyon Press, www.copper canyonpress.org.

Cathy Smith Bower's poem "The Love" from *The Love That Ended Yesterday in Texas* (Iris Press 1997). Copyright © 1992, 1997 by Cathy Smith Bowers. Her poem "Peace Lillies" from *A Book of Minutes* (Iris Press 2004). Copyright © 2004 by Cathy Smith Bowers. Her poem "Whistle-Speak" from *The Candle I Hold Up To See You* (Iris Press 2008). Copyright © 2008 by Cathy Smith Bowers. All three poems reprinted with the permission of Iris Press, Oak Ridge, Tennessee.

Steven Cramer's poem "Everyone Who Left Us" from *Goodbye to the Orchard* (Sarabande Books 2004). Copyright © 2004 by Steven Cramer. Reprinted with the permission of the author.

J.P. Dancing Bear's poem "A Brief Informal History" first appeared in *Alehouse*. Reprinted with the permission of the author.

Carol Dine's poem "Owl's Head" from in *Places in the Bone* (Rutgers University Press 2005). Reprinted with the permission of the author.

Rita Dove's poem "Fox Trot Fridays" from *American Smooth* (W. W. Norton & Company 2004). Copyright © 2004 by Rita Dove. Used by permission of W. W. Norton & Company, Inc.

Carol Ann Duffy's poem "Mrs. Lazarus" from *The World's Wife: Poems by Carol Ann Duffy* (Faber & Faber 1999). Copyright © 1999 by Carol Ann Duffy. Reprinted with the permission of Picador, London.

Douglas Dunn's poem "Kaleidoscope" from his Whitbread Prize winning book of poems *Elegies* (Faber & Faber 1985). Copyright © 1985 by Douglas Dunn. Reprinted with the permission of Faber & Faber, Ltd., London.

Gail Rudd Entrekin's poem "Michelle" first appeared in *Nevada County Poetry Series 2005 Anthology*. Her poem "Wailing" from *Change (Will Do You Good)* (Poetic Matrix Press 2005). Both poems Copyright © 2005 by Gail Rudd Entrekin. Reprinted with the permission of the author.

Joseph Enzweiler's poem "The Immense" from *A Curb in Eden* (Iris Press 2003). Copyright © 1999, 2003 by Joseph Enzweiler. Reprinted with the permission of Iris Press, Oak Ridge, Tennessee.

R. G. Evans' poem "Many Feet Going" first published in *Sow's Ear Review*. Reprinted with the permission of the author.

György Faludy's poem, excerpted from "Farewell to Recsk" and translated

315

316

Thérése Halscheid's poem "Peasants Around Small Fires" from *Without Home* (Kells Books 2001). Copyright © 2001 by Thérése Halscheid. Reprinted with the permission of the author.

Diane Holland's poem "At Baggage Claim" from *The Hand That Stayed From Its Desire* (Predator Press 2006). Copyright © 2006 by Diane Holland. Reprinted with the permission of the author.

Liu Hongbin's poems "Sprit of the Sea" and "The Unfamiliar Customs House" from *A Day Within Days* (Ambit Books 2006). Copyright © 2006 by Liu Hongbin. Reprinted with the permission of Ambit Books, London.

Faye J. Hoops' poem "Parade" first appeared in *The Reach of Song Anthology* (Georgia Poetry Society 1997). Reprinted with the permission of the author.

Betty Lynch Husted's poem "Salvage Anthropology" first published in *RondeDance 1*, March 2006. Reprinted with the permission of the author.

Major Jackson's poems "Urban Renewal XIII" and "Allegheny" from *Hoops* (W.W. Norton & Co. 2006). Copyright © 2006 by Major Jackson. Reprinted with the permission of the author.

Liesl Jobson's poem "Missive from Skakaland" first appeared in *The Mad Hatters' Review* and *Dragonfire*. Reprinted with the permission of the author.

Ilya Kaminsky's poem "Author's Prayer" from *Dancing in Odessa* (Tupelo Press 2004). Copyright © 2004 by Ilya Kaminsky. Reprinted with the permission of Tupelo Press, Dorset, Vermont.

Sándor Kányádi's poem "Wartime," translated from Hungarian by Paul Sohar, appeared in English in *Dancing Embers* (Twisted Spoon Press 2002). Copyright © 2002 by Paul Sohar. Reprinted with the permission of the author and Mr. Sohar.

Willie James King's poem "Old Cahawba" has appeared in the following journals: *The Black River Review, Crazyquilt Quarterly,* and *Riverrun,* and in

by Thomas Lux. His poem "Criss Cross Apple Sauce" from *New and Selected Poems: 1975-1995* (Houghton Mifflin Company 1997). Copyright © 1997 by Thomas Lux. Both poems reprinted by permission of Houghton Mifflin Company. All Rights Reserved.

Rebecca McClanahan's poems "Lament," "First Husband," "Never, Ever," "The Other Woman," and "There Are Days" from *Deep Light: New and Selected Poems 1997-2007* (Iris Press 2007). Copyright © 2007 by Rebecca McClanahan. Reprinted with the permission of Iris Press, Oak Ridge, Tennessee.

Jim McGarrah's poem "March Is the Cruelest Month" first appeared in the inaugural issue of *Unbound Press Magazine* in 2007. Reprinted with the permission of the author.

Jenni Meredith's poem "Vertical Blinds" was first published on a CD-ROM produced by Mental Health Media in association with The Moving Page Company, London, England. Copyright © 2002 by Jenni Meredith. Reprinted with the permission of the author.

Susan Meyers' poem "That Year" from *Keep and Give Away* (University of South Carolina 2006). Copyright © 2007 by Susan Meyers. Reprinted with the permission of the University of South Carolina Press.

Joseph Mills' poem "Recipe" from *Somewhere During the Spin Cycle* (Press 53 2006). Copyright © 2006 by Joseph Mills. Reprinted with the permission of the author.

Barbara Mitchell's poem "Small Courage" first appeared in *Prairie Messenger* in 2001. Reprinted with the permission of the author.

Majid Naficy's poems "To the Children of Prison and Exile" and "Ah, Los Angeles" are revised from those in his book *Muddy Shoes* (Beyond Baroque Books 1999). Copyright © 1999 by Majid Naficy. Reprinted with the permission of the author.

Kevin Simmonds' poem "After Katrina" was first published in *Callaloo*, Fall 2006. Reprinted with the permission of the author.

Marcia Slatkin's poem "A Late Blessing" from *I Kidnap My Mother* (Finishing Line Press 2005). Copyright © 2005 by Marcia Slatkin. Reprinted with the permission of the author and Finishing Line Press, Georgetown, Kentucky.

Satyendra Srivastava's poems "Sir Winston Churchill Knew My Mother" and "The Resolve" and "The Most Satisfying Moment" from *Sir Winston Churchill Knew My Mother* (Ambit Books 2006). Copyright © 2006 by Satyendra Srivastava. Reprinted with the permission of Ambit Books, London.

William Stafford's poem "A Memorial: Son Bret" Copyright © 1993, 1998 by the Estate of William Stafford. Reprinted from *The Way It Is: New & Selected Poems* with the permission of Graywolf Press, Saint Paul, Minnesota.

Dennis Ward Stiles' poem "Bringing You Back" was published in *The Poetry Society of South Carolina 1999 Yearbook* as the Lyric Poem Prize winner. Reprinted with the permission of the author.

Becky Thompson's poem "Post-Attica Visit" first appeared in the anthology *Warpland: A Journal of Black Literature and Ideas*, Vol. 12, No. 1, 2005. Copyright 2005 © by Becky Thompson. Reprinted with the permission of the author.

Rhett Iseman Trull's poem "Counting Miracles at the State Asylum" first appeared in the online journal *Liturgical Credo*. Reprinted with the permission of the author.

Brian Turner's poems "2000 lbs.," "Night in Blue," and "To Sand" from *Here, Bullet* (Alice James Books 2005). Copyright © 2005 by Brian Turner. Reprinted with the permission of Alice James Books, Farmington, Maine.

Susan M. Varon's poem "Poem to My Right Hand" first appeared in *Bellevue Literary Review*, Vol 7 No. 1. Reprinted with the permission of the author.

321

Contributors' Biographies

Anthony S. Abbott was born in San Francisco. His poems have appeared in numerous magazines and journals including *New England Review*, *Southern Poetry Review*, *St. Andrews Review*, *Pembroke*, *Tar River Poetry*, *Theology Today*, and *Anglican Theological Review*. His first book of poems, *The Girl in the Yellow Raincoat* (St. Andrews Press 1989) was nominated for the Pulitzer Prize. His poetry collections include *A Small Thing Like A Breath* (St. Andrews Press 1993), *The Search for Wonder in the Cradle of the World* (St. Andrews Press 2001), and *The Man Who* (Main Street Rag 2005). In 2003 his first novel, *Leaving Maggie Hope*, won the Novello Award and was published by Novello Festival Press. The novel won the Gold Award from ForeWord Magazine in the literary fiction category. His poem in this anthology, "The Man Who Speaks to His Daughter on Her 40th Birthday," is addressed to his daughter Carolyn who died just before her fourth birthday from encephalitis.

Paul Allen teaches poetry writing and writing song lyrics at The College of Charleston in Charleston, South Carolina. Published in numerous journals and anthologies, his work includes *American Crawl* (Vassar Miller Poetry Prize, University of North Texas Press 1997) and the chapbook, *His Longing: The Small Penis Oratorio* (FootHills Publishing, Kanona, New York 2005), a sequence of metaphysical conceits which deal with the concept that all of us feel we don't quite measure up, especially spiritually. His essay, "Juice," appears in *Pushcart Prize XXXII: Best of the Small Presses, 2008*. Of his poem in this anthology, "Lapses," Mr. Allen writes: "Recovery, it seems, is a life's work, not a goal. The goal is peace and full forgiveness of ourselves and of others. Part of that forgiveness is forgiving ourselves for not having reached the stage of recovery we want. And there are plenty of reminders that we haven't. 'Enough of that,' Yeats says, 'Better to smile on all that smile.' And so we keep dancing, despite the measure we missed."

Doug Anderson has written two books of poetry, *The Moon Reflected Fire* (Alice James Books 1994), which won the Kate Tufts Discovery Award, and *Blues for Unemployed Secret Police* (Curbstone Press 2000). His poems have been widely anthologized and have appeared in many distinguished literary journals. He has received grants from the National Endowment for the Arts, the American Academy of Poets, and other funding organizations and has won many prizes, including a Pushcart Prize for 2005. He has also written plays, screenplays and criticism, and has just finished a memoir, *Don't Rub Your Eyes*, about the Vietnam War and the 1960s.

Simon Armitage, widely considered the most popular contemporary British poet, has published nine volumes of poetry including *Killing Time* (1999), *Selected Poems* (2001), *The Universal Home Doctor* (2002), and *Travelling Songs* (2002), all published by Faber & Faber. His latest collection of poems is *Tyrannosaurus Rex Versus the Corduroy Kid* (Faber and Faber 2006). *The Shout*, a book of new and selected poems, was published in the U.S. in April 2005 by Harcourt. He has received numerous awards for his poetry including the Sunday Times Author of the Year, one of the first Forward Prizes, and a Lannan Award. He writes for radio, television and film, and is the author of four stage plays, including *Mister Heracles*, a version of the Euripides play *The Madness of Heracles*. His recent dramatization of *The Odyssey*, commissioned by the BBC, was broadcast on Radio 4 in 2004 and is available through BBC Worldwide. His two novels, *Little Green Man* (2001) and *The White Stuff* (2004) were published by Penguin. Armitage has taught at the University of Leeds and the University of Iowa's Writers' Workshop, and is currently a senior lecturer at Manchester Metropolitan University. With Robert Crawford, he edited *The Penguin Anthology of Poetry from Britain and Ireland Since 1945*. Other anthologies include *Short and Sweet — 101 Very Short Poems*, and a selection of Ted Hughes' poetry, both published by Faber & Faber. He is currently working on a translation of the middle English classic poem *Sir Gawain and the Green Knight*, commissioned by Faber & Faber in the UK and Norton in the US.

Bernardo Atxaga was born in Asteasu, Gipuzkoa, Basque Country, in

1951, and belongs to the group of Basque writers who began publishing in their mother tongue, Euskera, in the 1970s. He graduated in economics from the University of the Basque Country and later studied philosophy at Barcelona University. His first poetry collection, *Etiopia* (1978) received the Spanish Critics' Prize in Basque Language. *Etiopia* has been translated into Spanish, French, Finnish, and Italian, which won the Cesare Pavese Prize. Translations of his poetry have appeared throughout Europe and the Americas, and he's considered to be the most internationally renowned Basque author. His novel *Obabakoak*, published in 1988, won the Spanish Premio Nacional de Narrative in 1989, and has been translated into more than 25 languages.

Rachel Tzvia Back, poet, translator, and professor of literature, was born in the US and has lived in Israel for the last 28 years. Her poetry collections include *Azimuth* (Sheep Meadow Press 2001) and *The Buffalo Poems* (Duration Press 2002) and *On Ruins and Return* (Shearsman Books 2007). Back is the author of the critical monograph *Led by Language: the Poetry and Poetics of Susan Howe* (University of Alabama Press 2000). Her translations of the poetry of pre-eminent Hebrew poet Lea Goldberg in *Lea Goldberg: Selected Poetry and Drama* (Toby Press 2005) were awarded a 2005 PEN Translation grant. Back teaches at Oranim College and Bar-Ilan University and lives in Galilee, in the north of Israel.

Carole Baldock is proud owner of three children, all in good working order; two cats, need slight attention; a computer; and a B.A. Hons. from Liverpool John Moores University. Widely-published: non-fiction, poetry and prose, with enough poems over the years to fill a drawer. Her pamphlet, *Bitching* (Sound Publications 2002), is now in its second edition. Her first full collection was *Give Me Where to Stand* (Headland 2007). Other books include *Writing Reviews* (How To Books 1996), *Making Money From Writing* (Sound Publications 2008), and *How To Raise Confident Children* (Sheldon Press 2000). Formerly Coordinator of Liverpool's Dead Good Poets Society, she is now Editor of *Competitions Bulletin* as well as *Orbis*, a renowned international literary journal of over 30 years' standing. Of her poem in this anthology, "Now that May Is Here," Baldock writes, "The title is a little contradictory; Keats was longing to be in England, which implies homesickness when this is the opposite, a strange mixture of wanderlust and nostalgia, in the sense of yearning for a past holiday, mostly when it feels as if the chance can never come again. And missing your children. However, though I must confess that I am not really plagued by this because writing concentrates the mind so much, yet when I do miss them it hits twice as hard."

Mary Jo Bang is author of five books of poetry including *Louise in Love* (Grove Press 2001), *The Eye Like a Strange Balloon* (Grove Press 2004), *The Downstream Extremity of the Isle of Swans* (University of Georgia Press 2001), and *Apology for Want* (Middlebury 1997). She lives in St. Louis, Missouri, where she is a Professor of English and Director of the Creative Writing Program at Washington University. Her poem "You Were You Are Elegy" is from her most recent book *Elegy* (Graywolf Press 2007), winner of the 2007 National Book Critics Circle Award. *Elegy* chronicles the year following the death of her 37-year-old son Michael Donner Van Hook in 2004. He died of an accidental prescription drug overdose, according to the *St. Louis Post-Dispatch*.

Georgia Ann Banks–Martin was born in Lincoln Park, Michigan, and currently resides in Montgomery, Alabama. She received her M.F.A. in Creative Writing from Queens University of Charlotte and has had poems published recently in *Möbius*, *Thanal Online*, and *Poetic Hours*.

Jennifer Barber is the author of *Rigging the Wind* (Kore Press 2003) and the recipient of a 2004 Pushcart Prize. Her poetry has appeared in anthologies such as *Four Way Reader #2* (Four Way Books) and *Take Three: 3* (Graywolf Press) and in a number of literary journals, including *Field, Fulcrum, Upstreet, Harvard Review,* and *Agni*. She is the founding and current editor of the literary journal *Salamander,* published at Suffolk University in Boston, where she teaches literature and writing.

Shaindel Beers is currently a professor of English at Blue Mountain Community College in Pendleton, Oregon. Her poetry, fiction, and social commentary have appeared in *Willow Review, Poetry Miscellany, Hunger Mountain*, and other journals. She serves as poetry editor of *Contrary* magazine. Of her poem in this anthology, "A Study in Weights and Measures," she writes: "I feel that this poem expresses various stages of recovery, which aren't necessarily linear—the instinct to fight sometimes feels like too much, and this is followed by a fleeting thought that it would be easier to surrender. Nothing that I know of dissipates this impulse like seeing others fight. The need to emulate them becomes your support."

Nazand Begikhani was born in Kurdistan, Iraq, in 1964. She has been living in exile (Denmark, France, and the U.K.) since 1987. She took her first degree in English language and literature, then completed an M.A. and Ph.D. in comparative literature at the Sorbonne. She published her first poetry collection *Yesterday of Tomorrow* in Paris in 1995. Her second and third collections were published in Kurdistan by Arras: *Celebrations* (2004) and *Colour of Sand* (2005). *Bells of Speech* (Ambit Books 2007), from which her poems in this anthology have been reprinted, is her first collection written in English. Begkhani is a polyglot who translates her own poetry into French and English, and her poems have also been translated into Arabic and Persian. She has also translated Baudelaire and T.S. Eliot into Kurdish. Begikhani is a founding member and coordinator of Kurdish Women Action Against Honor Killing. Her research into Kurdish gender issues is widely published in Kurdish, French, and English.

Pam Bernard, poet and painter, received her B.A. from Harvard University in History of Art and her M.F.A. in creative writing from the Graduate Program for Writers at Warren Wilson. Bernard teaches creative writing at Emerson College and also at New Hampshire Community Technical College. Her most recent awards are a second Massachusetts Cultural Council Fellowship in poetry, a National Endowment for the Arts Fellowship in creative writing and a MacDowell Fellowship. She has published two full-length collections of poetry—*My Own Hundred Doors* (Bright Hill Press 1996) and *Across the Dark* (Main Street Rag 2007)—and her poems have appeared in *TriQuarterly, Spoon River Review, Prairie*

Schooner, *Salamander*, *Yankee Magazine*, and other journals. Ms. Bernard lives in Walpole, New Hampshire. Her poem "[As the landscape turns melancholic]" is from *Blood Garden: an elegy for Raymond*, a forthcoming collection from WordTech Turning Point Editions about her father's experiences as an infantryman in World War I.

Elizabeth Bernardin has published poems in *The South Carolina Poetry Society Yearbook 2007*, *Kakalak 2007*, *The Southern Poetry Anthology, Volume I: South Carolina*, *Notre Dame Review*, *The Devil's Millhopper*, and *Negative Capability*. She lives in Georgetown, South Carolina. Of her poem in this anthology, "Catharine's Book," she writes: "I came upon the book, read the words Catharine had written and was so moved by the notion that her love had left for his assignment without saying goodbye. I imagined Catharine trying to find him at the station. Holding the book in my hands touched my own sadness at the time, over my husband's death a few years earlier. I thought about my husband and how I missed our old life together. Sometimes we hold on to grief when we need to let it go. I think I began to fully let my past go during writing the poem. The words, the book of poems, writing my own poem helped me to release my own sadness."

Sonja Besford is one of four sisters born in Belgrade. Her three sisters still live there but Sonja moved to Britain as a student and was trapped into a marriage, without even being pregnant. She lives in London and visits Belgrade frequently. Apart from her work as a playwright and critic, Besford has published six books, including a novel and a collection of short stories, and poetry. Her seventh book, *memories of summers in brist near gradac and other poems* (Ambit Books 2006), where her poem "subjects in the cold winter of '93/'94 belgrade" appeared, was written in English and is dedicated to a class of Belgrade children of whom she and her new husband have been patrons for the last eight years.

Laurel Blossom's book-length narrative prose poem, *Degrees of Latitude*, was published by Four Way Books in November 2007. Her most recent book of lyric poetry is *Wednesday: New and Selected Poems* (Ridgeway Press 2004). Earlier books include *The Papers Said* (Greenhouse Review Press

1993), *What's Wrong* (Cobham & Hatherton Press 1987), and *Any Minute* (Greenhouse Review Press 1979). Her work has appeared in a number of anthologies, including *180 More: Extraordinary Poems for Every Day*, edited by Billy Collins (Random House 2005), and in national journals including *Poetry*, *The American Poetry Review*, *Pequod*, *The Paris Review*, *The Carolina Quarterly*, *Deadsnake Apotheosis*, *Many Mountains Moving*, *Seneca Review*, and *Harper's*, among others. Her poetry has been nominated for both the Pushcart Prize and the Elliston Prize. Blossom is the editor of *Splash! Great Writing About Swimming* (Ecco Press 1996) and *Many Lights in Many Windows: Twenty Years of Great Fiction and Poetry from The Writers Community* (Milkweed Editions 1997). She serves on the editorial board of *Heliotrope: a journal of poetry*. Blossom has received fellowships from the National Endowment for the Arts, the New York Foundation for the Arts, the Ohio Arts Council, and Harris Manchester College (Oxford University), where she serves on the Board of Regents. She co-founded The Writers Community, the esteemed writing residency and advanced workshop program of the YMCA National Writer's Voice. Blossom belongs to The Explorers Club and the Circumnavigators Club in New York City. She lives in rural South Carolina.

David Bottoms was born in 1949 in Canton, Georgia. His most recent work includes *Waltzing Through the Endtime* (Copper Canyon Press 2004), *Vagrant Grace* (Copper Canyon Press 1999), *Armored Hearts: Selected and New Poems* (Copper Canyon Press 1995) and the novel *Easter Weekend* (Washington Square Press 1990). His first collection, *Shooting Rats at the Bibb County Dump* (W. Morrow 1980), was selected by Robert Penn Warren for the 1979 Walt Whitman Award. His poems have appeared in many magazines, including *The Atlantic Monthly, Harper's, The Kenyon Review, The New Yorker, The Paris Review*, and *The Southern Review*. He also serves as editor for *Five Points* literary magazine. His honors include a Guggenheim Fellowship, the Levinson Prize, an Ingram-Merrill Award, an American Academy and Institute of Arts and Letters Award, and a National Endowment for the Arts Fellowship. Bottoms is currently the Poet Laureate of Georgia and holds the Amos Distinguished Chair in English Letters at Georgia State University.

Cathy Smith Bowers was born and reared, one of six children, in the small mill town of Lancaster, South Carolina. She received her B.A. and M.A.T. in English at Winthrop University in Rock Hill, South Carolina. She went on to do graduate work in Modern British Poetry at Oxford University in England. Her poems have appeared widely in publications such as *The Atlantic Monthly, The Georgia Review, Poetry, The Southern Review*, and *The Kenyon Review*. She is a winner of The General Electric Award for Younger Writers, recipient of a South Carolina Poetry Fellowship, and winner of The South Carolina Arts Commission Fiction Project. She served for many years as poet-in-residence at Queens University of Charlotte where she received the 2002 J.B. Fuqua Distinguished Educator Award. She now teaches in the Queens low-residency M.F.A. program. Smith Bowers is the author of four collections of poetry: *The Love That Ended Yesterday in Texas* (Texas Tech University Press 1992), *Traveling in Time of Danger* (Iris Press 1999), *A Book of Minutes* (Iris Press 2004), and *The Candle I Hold Up To See You* (Iris Press 2008).

Renée Michele Breeden began her affair with writing at the age of 10 during her language arts class. From the age of 10 to her present age of 34, she has birthed thousands of unpublished jewels. She has facilitated three spoken word shows that include *Dinner and a Poem*, *Poetry at Perks*, and *Wise Words Wednesdays*, as well as working in conjunction with Anthony "Da Boogieman" Rucker on the workshop series *Liquid Language* at the Seventh Avenue Barnes & Noble in Brooklyn, New York's Park Slope. Another poetry show is in gestation. Renée is a Cave Canem workshop series participant with Kate Rushin and Patricia Smith. She is presently working on a book of poems as well as her first novel. Of her poem in this anthology, "Original Sin," she writes: "I wrote this poem for 'the other woman'—the woman who battles with her own set of emotions and the torment of being in love with a man who is married to someone else. It was written for the moment the woman realizes that what she needs is more than what he can offer, and it is the first step to forgiving herself."

Jericho Brown holds a Ph.D. in literature and creative writing from the University of Houston. His poems have appeared or are forthcoming in *AGNI*, *jubilat*, *New England Review*, *Prairie Schooner*, and many other journals and anthologies, including the Cave Canem anthology *Gathering Ground*, edited by Toi Derricote and Cornelius Eady (University of Michigan 2006). His first book, *Please*, will be published by Western Michigan University's New Issues Poetry & Prose in the Fall of 2008, and he is an Assistant Professor of English at the University of San Diego. Of his poem in this anthology, he writes: "In terms of recovery, 'Because My Name Is Jericho' seems to me a comment on invisibility and anonymity and the ways in which some of us love to confuse these with masculinity."

Walter Brueggemann, Ph.D., is an Old Testament scholar and author. He is an advocate and practitioner of rhetorical criticism who has written hundreds of articles and commentaries as well as 60 books, including *Finally Comes the Poet* (Fortress Press 1989), in which he proposes preaching that is artistic, poetic, and dramatic. This type of preaching, in Dr. Brueggemann's view, enables a preacher to forge communion in the midst of alienation, bring healing out of guilt, and empower the listener's imagination. Dr. Brueggemann proposed poetic preaching as an alternative to theological/homiletical discourse that is moralistic, pietistic, or overly scholarly. *Finally Comes the Poet* was the basis for the 1989 Lyman Beecher Lectures at Yale Divinity School. Born in Tilden, Nebraska in 1933, he was the son of a United Church of Christ minister, who instilled in him the artistry as well as the authority of scripture. Dr. Brueggemann received an A.B. from Elmhurst College, a B.D. from Eden Theological Seminary, a Th.D. from Union Theological Seminary, New York, and Ph.D. from Saint Louis University. He was professor of Old Testament and Dean at Eden Theological Seminary, St. Louis, Missouri. Beginning in 1986, he served as William Marcellus McPheeters Professor of Old Testament at Columbia Theological Seminary, Decatur, Georgia, where he is now professor emeritus. He still resides in Decatur, Georgia.

Clinton B. Campbell's work has appeared in periodicals and anthologies including *MARGIE, California Quarterly, Passager, Writer's Digest* and *Journal of New Jersey Poets*. His poem, "Club Soda Nights," was published in *Using Poetry in Therapeutic Settings: A Resource Manual & Poetry Collection*

(2000), compiled by the Vital Signs Poetry Project of the Children's Inn at the National Institutes of Health, Bethesda, MD. His work is also in *The Cancer Poetry Project*, and his poem, "My Veteran's Day Prayer" was entered into the *Congressional Record* by Congressman Joe Wilson on 11/ 9/07. Campbell lives in Beaufort, South Carolina with his wife, photographer/poet Karen M. Peluso. Of his poem in this anthology, "Club Soda Nights," Campbell writes: "The poem came from my early days of recovery when giving up the old ways was difficult. I was at a party playing the 'poor me' act when someone said, 'You are more fun when you are drinking.' That line was the scaffolding for the poem because it never made the last draft. The poem took 14 years to write. Even though that party was 25 years ago, being sober is still One Day at a Time, and when things are tough it's down to an hour or a minute at a time, like the poem's final line, 'and we take the long way home'—slow down, take a deep breath and take time to smell the roses."

Margaret Chula is a poet, teacher, and performer. From 1980-1992, she lived in Kyoto, Japan, where she taught English at Doshisha Women's College and studied *ikebana*, woodblock printing, and practiced Zen. Her five collections of poetry including *Grinding My Link*, which received the Haiku Society of Americas Book Award. Her poem in this anthology, "Equilibrium," is from a collaborative project with quilt artist Cathy Erickson. Their book *What Remains: Japanese Americans in Internment Camps*, was released in 2007. About the poem, Chula writes: "Following the attack by the Japanese Imperial Navy on Pearl Harbor on December 7, 1941, President Roosevelt signed Executive Order 9066 that led to the detention of 110,000 Japanese Americans, who were eventually incarcerated in internment camps located in remote desert areas until the end of World War II. How do you recover from suddenly being forced to leave your home, possessions, businesses, and friends, not knowing where you're going or how long you'll be gone? From the injustice of being imprisoned in barracks surrounded by barbed wire? From the humiliation of being unemployed and idle after you had been a respected member of the community? The man and his family in 'Equilibrium' eschew the justifiable reactions of anger, victimization, and retaliation.

Accepting their situation, they set to work creating objects of beauty and usefulness—learning how to straighten their backs and be proud."

Allison Adelle Hedge Coke was born between paternal oratory and sudden maternal madness; somewhere north of the condor and south of raven. Crow sometimes cawed morning into malady's mixture, pouring song and hack into bleating skies, swirling sunrise and set. Once, high over the arctic, she witnessed the pounding lights hammer horizon. Since that time her rendezvous with realtime has been a real ride. Hedge Coke is Huron and Cherokee, a MacDowell Fellow, and holds the Distinguished Paul W. Reynolds and Clarice Kingston Reynolds Endowed Chair in English as an Associate Professor of Poetry and Writing at the University of Nebraska, Kearney. She is a core faculty in the University of Nebraska M.F.A. Program and current Visiting Faculty of the M.F.A. Intensive Programs at University of California, Palm Desert and Naropa University. Her books include: *Dog Road Woman* (Coffee House Press 1997), which won the American Book Award, *The Year of the Rat*, a chapbook, (Grimes Press 2000), *Rock Ghost, Willow, Deer* (University of Nebraska Press 2004), *Off-Season City Pipe* (Coffee House Press 2005), *Blood Run* (Salt Publications U.K. 2006-U.S. 2007), and *To Topos Ahani: Indigenous American Poetry* (Oregon State University 2007). Of her poem in this anthology, "Remembrance," she writes, "It is traditional, when a close loved one passes, to remember them in a creative work: song, story, poem, artwork, or other artistic vessel for many Indigenous peoples of the Americas. Thus, a survivor's mourning heals through the process of acknowledgment and remembering while creating a legacy force from the memory of life and witnessing the mourning process. '*Wokiksuye*' is this remembrance for the one true love of my life. He spoke Lakota, thus when speaking to him over significant matters, I would as well. The process of crossing over and mourning is absolutely significant, so herein the language represents this respect."

Martha Collins is the author of the book-length poem *Blue Front* (Graywolf 2006), which focuses on a lynching her father witnessed when he was five years old. *Blue Front* won an Anisfield-Wolf Award, as well as an Ohioana Award, and was chosen as one of the "25 Books to Remember from 2006" by the New York Public Library. Collins has published four earlier collections of poems and a chapbook, and two collections of co-translations of poetry from the Vietnamese.

Peter Cooley has published seven books of poetry, six of them with Carnegie-Mellon University press, which just released his most recent collection *Divine Margins*. He has recent poems in *New Letters*, *Southwest Review*, *Ploughshares*, *Third Coast*, *MARGIE*, and *Literary Imagination*. He is Professor of English and Director of Creative Writing at Tulane University in New Orleans. Of his poem in this anthology, "A Place Made of Starlight," he writes: "This title poem from my book unlocked a good deal of personal history which, in conjunction with psychotherapy, allowed me to remember and forgive the past. I could only write this poem, whose sestina form evoked the obsessive nature of abuse and memory and recovery, once my mother, father, and sister had died, as they each did in 2000. I hope the sestina form allows for a musical relief from the concerns of the subject matter."

Genie Cotner's poems have appeared in journals and anthologies including *Kakalak 2007: An Anthology of Carolina Poets*, *Iodine Poetry Journal*, *Main Street Rag*, and *Only Connect: The Charlotte Writers' Club Anthology Volume 3*. She was the 2007 winner of the Deane Ritch Lomax Poetry Contest. She lives in Charlotte, North Carolina. Of her poem in this anthology, "*Ikebana*," she writes: "The poem speaks to my physical and emotional recovery from jaw cancer and years of reconstructive surgery. Poetry has been a godsend to me, a source of connection in difficult times."

Steven Cramer is the author of four poetry collections: *The Eye that Desires to Look Upward* (Galileo Press 1987), *The World Book* (Copper Beach 1992), *Dialogue for the Left and Right Hand* (Brookline Books 1997), and *Goodbye to the Orchard*, (Sarabande Books 2004), which won the 2005 Sheila Motton Prize from the New England Poetry Club, and was named a 2005 Honor Book in Poetry by the Massachusetts Center for the Book. His poems and criticism have appeared in numerous literary journals, including *The Atlantic Monthly, The Nation, The New Republic, The Paris Review, Partisan Review, Poetry,* and *TriQuarterly*; as well as in *The Autumn House Anthology of Contemporary American Poets* and *The POETRY Anthology, 1912-2002.* He has taught literature and writing at Bennington College, Boston University, M.I.T., and Tufts University. Recipient of fellowships from the Massachusetts Artists Foundation and the National Endowment for the Arts, he currently directs the Low-Residency M.F.A. Program in Creative Writing at Lesley University in Cambridge, Massachusetts.

J. P. Dancing Bear is the author of *Gacela of Narcissus City* (Main Street Rag 2006), *Billy Last Crow* (Turning Point 2004), *What Language* (Slipstream 2002), and *Conflicted Light* (SalmonPoetry 2008). His poems have been published in *Shenandoah, Poetry International, New Orleans Review, National Poetry Review, Marlboro Review, Mississippi Review* and many others. He is the editor of the *American Poetry Journal* and the host of "Out of Our Minds" a weekly poetry program on public radio station KKUP, Cupertino, California.

Shelley Davidow was born in Johannesburg, South Africa in 1969. She completed a Bachelor's degree in English and Drama at Wits University, and in 1991 she achieved recognition for her young adult novel *Freefalling* in the national Maskew Miller Longman Young Africa Award. She has lived and worked in South Africa, Zimbabwe, England, Germany, Qatar and the U.S. She has published a variety of books, ranging from children's readers for Africa and the Caribbean, to young adult literature and adult non-fiction. She co-wrote the biography *My Life with AIDS: Charmayne Broadway's Story* (Southern Books, South Africa 1998). Recently she was nominated for the 2002 African Writer's Prize for her young adult novel *In the Shadow of Inyangani* (Macmillan 2003). Her poetry has been anthologized in *Oregon Poets Against the War, Imagining Ourselves,* and *In Our Own Words: A Generation Defining Itself.* Her memoir, *The Eye of the Moon* (Rainy Nights Press 2007), describes her coming of age set against the backdrop of Southern Africa. She now lives in Sarasota, Florida, with her husband and son. Of her poem in this anthology, "Hemispheres," she writes: "I was born and grew up in South Africa, where the water goes down the drain the other way. At the age of 34, after being in America for 4 years, I was diagnosed with a pituitary tumor. I suffered loss of vision and other nastiness. Part of the recovery process, for me, was going back in my imagination, to the place and time before anything was amiss, reliving the bittersweet, paradoxical memories of my early years, when my body was whole. I'm positive that geography plays a big part in healing, and the memory of a healthy Self can help recreate an actual healthy Self again. The poem is a dissolution of space and time, an attempt to make some kind of peace with a new hemisphere, while simultaneously living into another one, where all was whole, and well."

Nehassaiu deGannes work has appeared or is forthcoming in *American Poetry Review*, *Callaloo*, *Poem / Memoir / Story*, *Encyclopedia Project, Tuesday Journal* and *Painted Bride Quarterly*. She received the 2008 Poetry Fellowship from the Rhode Island State Council for the Arts, and in 2001 Michael Harper selected her poems for the Philbrick Poetry Prize for New England poets. She is a Cave Canem Fellow and divides her time between Providence and New York. Of her poem in this anthology, "Last Surviving Hymn to Hathor," she writes, "I foraged among the blues and sacred myth to incant a recovery from the losses of innocence and trust engendered by domestic violence."

Carol Dine's book of poems on Vincent Van Gogh will be published in 2008 by The Bitter Oleander Press. Her memoir *Places in the Bone* (Rutgers University Press 2005), which combines prose and poetry, received positive reviews in *Publisher'sWeekly*, *Library Journal*, and *ForeWord Magazine*. Author of two collections of poetry, her work appears in literary magazines including *Blue Mesa Review*, *Puerto del Sol*, *Prairie Schooner*, and *Salamander*. The subject of her poem in this anthology, "Owl's Head," is the death of her lover at the age of 40. She says, "The poem made my love tangible and was a way to control memory and my grief."

Rita Dove served as Poet Laureate of the United States and Consultant to the Library of Congress from 1993 to 1995 and as Poet Laureate of the Commonwealth of Virginia from 2004 to 2006. She has received numerous literary and academic honors, among them the 1987 Pulitzer Prize in Poetry. Dove was born in Akron, Ohio in 1952. She received her M.F.A. from the University of Iowa. She also held a Fulbright scholarship at the Universität

Tübingen in Germany. She has published the poetry collections *The Yellow House on the Corner* (Carnegie-Mellon University Press 1980), *Museum* (Carmichael and Carmichael 1983), *Thomas and Beulah* (Carnegie-Mellon University Press 1986), *Grace Notes* (W. W. Norton 1989), *Selected Poems* (Vintage 1993), *Mother Love* (W. W. Norton 1995), *On the Bus with Rosa Parks* (W. W. Norton 1999), a book of short stories, *Fifth Sunday* (University of Virginia Press 1985), the novel *Through the Ivory Gate* (Pantheon 1992), essays under the title *The Poet's World* (Library of Congress 1995), and the play *The Darker Face of the Earth* (Story Line Press 1994), which had its world premiere in 1996 at the Oregon Shakespeare Festival and was subsequently produced at the Kennedy Center in Washington, D.C., the Royal National Theatre in London, and other theatres. *Seven for Luck*, a song cycle for soprano and orchestra with music by John Williams, was premiered by the Boston Symphony Orchestra at Tanglewood in 1998. For "America's Millennium," the White House's 1999/2000 New Year's celebration, Ms. Dove contributed — in a live reading at the Lincoln Memorial, accompanied by John Williams's music — a poem to Steven Spielberg's documentary *The Unfinished Journey*. She is the editor of *Best American Poetry 2000,* and from January 2000 to January 2002 she wrote a weekly column, "Poet's Choice," for *The Washington Post*. Her latest poetry collection, *American Smooth*, was published by W. W. Norton & Company in 2004. Rita Dove is Commonwealth Professor of English at the University of Virginia in Charlottesville, where she lives with her husband, the writer Fred Viebahn. Of her poems in *American Smooth*, including "Fox Trot Fridays," Ms. Dove has spoken of her desire to learn ballroom dance as part of the process of recovery after she and her husband's home burned to the ground.

Carol Ann Duffy, poet, playwright and freelance writer, was born in 1955 in Glasgow, Scotland. She grew up in Stafford, England, and she received an honors degree in philosophy from the University of Liverpool. She is a former editor of the literary magazine *Ambit* and is a regular reviewer and broadcaster. Her papers were acquired by the Robert W. Woodruff Library of Emory University in 1999, and in October 2000 she was awarded a five-year grant by the National Endowment for Science, Technology and the Arts. Her poetry collections include *Selling Manhattan*

(Anvil Press Poetry 1987), which won a Somerset Maugham Award, *Mean Time* (Anvil Press Poetry 1993), which won the Whitbread Poetry Award and the Forward Poetry Prize (Best Poetry Collection of the Year), *The World's Wife* (Faber & Faber 1999), and *Selected Poems* (Penguin Global 2004). *The Good Child's Guide to Rock N Roll* (Faber's Children's Books 2003) is the latest of her many books for children. Carol Ann Duffy is also an acclaimed playwright, and her plays have been performed at the Liverpool Playhouse and the Almeida Theatre in London. Her plays include *Take My Husband* (1982), *Cavern of Dreams* (1984), *Little Women, Big Boys* (1986) and *Loss* (1986), a radio play. She received an Eric Gregory Award in 1984 and a Cholmondeley Award in 1992 from the Society of Authors, the Dylan Thomas Award from the Poetry Society in 1989 and a Lannan Literary Award from the Lannan Foundation in 1995. She was awarded an Order of the British Empire in 1995, a Commander of the British Empire in 2001 and became a Fellow of the Royal Society of Literature in 1999. She moved from London to Manchester in 1996 and is Creative Director of the Writing School at Manchester Metropolitan University. Her latest collection of poetry is *Rapture* (Picador 2005).

Douglas Dunn was born in Inchinnan, Renfrewshire, Scotland, in 1942 and lived there until he married at the age of twenty-two. After working as a librarian in Scotland and Akron, Ohio, he studied English at Hull University, graduating in 1969. He then worked for eighteen months in the university library after which, in 1971, he became a freelance writer. In 1991 he was appointed Professor in the School of English at the University of St. Andrews. His 10 collections of poetry, including *Elegies* (Faber & Faber 1985), *The Year's Afternoon* and *The Donkey's Ears*, both from Faber & Faber in 2000, and *New and Selected 1964-1999* (Faber & Faber 2003). Dunn has written several radio and television plays, including *Ploughman's Share* and *Scotsman by Moonlight*. He has also edited *The Faber Book of Twentieth-Century Scottish Poetry* (2000). Douglas Dunn has won a Somerset Maugham Award, the Geoffrey Faber Memorial Prize, and has twice been awarded prizes by the Scottish Arts Council. In 1981 he was awarded the Hawthornden Prize for *St Kilda's Parliament* (Faber & Faber 1981). In January 1986 he was overall winner of the 1985 Whitbread

Book of the Year Award for his collection *Elegies*, which was written after the death of his wife, Lesley, from malignant melanoma.

Gail Rudd Entrekin teaches English and creative writing at Sierra College in Grass Valley, California. Her collections of poems include *Change (Will Do You Good)*, Slim Volume Series Selection for 2005 from Poetic Matrix Press, which was nominated for the California Book Awards; *You Notice the Body* (Hip Pocket Press 1998); and *John Danced* (Berkeley Poets Workshop & Press 1984). Poetry Editor of Hip Pocket Press since 2000, she edited *Sierra Songs & Descants: Poetry & Prose of the Sierra* in 2002 and *Six Sierra Poets*, released in 2007. Her poetry has been widely published in literary magazines and anthologies. She lives in Grass Valley, California with her husband, writer Charles Entrekin. Of her poems in this anthology, "Michele," and "Wailing," she writes: "These poems address the process of assimilating loss and other profound unchosen change into our lives and our world views and finding ways to go forward with hope."

Joseph Enzweiler was born in Cincinnati, Ohio in 1950. He received a degree in physics from Xavier University there, and moved to Fairbanks, Alaska in 1975. He received an M.S. in physics form the University of Alaska, Fairbanks, and in 1981 built a primitive log house in Goldstream Valley north of Fairbanks where he has lived ever since. He currently works as a carpenter, stone mason, and photographer during the summer and fall months, and spends his winters writing. Every few years he returns to rural northern Kentucky for several months where he lives with his brother and his family and is building a rock fence around his brother's three acres of land. Enzweiler has published four books of poetry: *Home Country* (Fire Weed Press 1986), *Stonework of the Sky* (Graywolf Press 1995), *A Curb in Eden* (Iris Press 2003), and *The Man Who Ordered Perch* (Iris Press 2004).

R.G. Evans' poems, fiction, and reviews have appeared in *Paterson Literary Review*, *Weird Tales*, *Alehouse*, *MARGIE*, and *Valparaiso Poetry Review*, among other publications. He holds an M.F.A. from Fairleigh Dickinson University, and he lives and teaches high school and college English in southern New Jersey. Of his poem in this anthology, "Many Feet Going," he writes: "Several years ago, I spent Christmas night reading *Waiting for Godot* ('Astride of a grave and a difficult birth. Down in the hole lingeringly, the gravedigger puts on the forceps'). A sobering, slapstick antidote for the season, but did this slice of absurdity feel like a first step toward recovery? The images of the parasol and the bright red nose in 'Many Feet Going' arose from Beckett's little Charlie Chaplin tramps, the pile of bones from the myths of Prometheus and Icarus. When I showed this poem to my friend and mentor Renee Ashley, her response was 'Boy, you *are* depressed.' Perhaps, but I'm still up here on the rope . . . still going . . ."

György Faludy (1910-2006) was born and died in Budapest, Hungary, but spent most of his long life in exile, first from Nazism and then Communism. But in between he got caught up in a Stalinist purge in Hungary in 1949 and languished for three years in a forced labor camp at Recsk where he nearly lost his life. As luck would have it, Stalin died first and Faludy was released from the dismantled gulag. His meditation of his experiences there and his miraculous survival resulted in his poem "Farewell to Recsk." An excerpt of this long poem appears in this anthology. In exile, Faludy kept in touch with his avid readers through Radio Free Europe. His poetry is a rare combination of aesthetism and philosophy.

Linda Annas Ferguson is the author of four collections of poetry: *Bird Missing from One Shoulder* (WordTech Editions 2007), *Stepping on Cracks in the Sidewalk* (Finishing Line Press 2006), *Last Chance to Be Lost* (Kentucky Writers' Coalition 2004), and *It's Hard to Hate a Broken Thing* (Palanquin Press, University of S.C. Aiken 2002). She was the 2005 Poetry Fellow for the South Carolina Arts Commission and served as the 2003-04 Poet-in-Residence for the Gibbes Museum of Art in Charleston, S.C. Her work is featured in the anthologies *Twenty: South Carolina Poetry Fellows* (Hub City Writers' Project 2005), *A Millennial Sampler of South Carolina Poetry* (Ninety-Six Press, Furman University 2005), *2006 Kakalak, an Anthology of Carolina Poets,* and *The Southern Poetry Anthology: South Carolina* (Texas Review Press 2007).

Annie Finch's books of poetry include *Calendars* (Tupelo Press 2003), a National Poetry Series finalist, *Eve* (Story Line Press 1997), *Home-Birth, The Encyclopedia of Scotland* (Salt Publishing 2004), *Catching the Mermother* (Aralia Press 1995), the epic poem *Marie Moving*, and a book of translations of the French Renaissance poet Louise Labé. Her book on poetics, *The Ghost of Meter* (University of Michigan Press 1993), has been reissued in paperback, and her anthology *A Formal Feeling Comes: Poems in Form by Contemporary Women* (Story Line Press 1994) is in its fifth printing. She is coeditor of *An Exaltation of Forms: Contemporary Poets Celebrate the Diversity of Their Art* (University of Michigan Press 2002), and her poems and translations have been published in the *Norton Anthology of World Poetry, Penguin Book of the Sonnet, The Kenyon Review, Poetry, Prairie Schooner, Field, The Paris Review, Agni Review, Thirteenth Moon, Partisan Review*, and elsewhere. She currently directs the Stonecoast Masters of Fine Arts program in creative writing at the University of Southern Maine.

Kate Gale received her doctorate in English from Claremont Graduate University. She teaches opera at California Institute of Arts and is Humanities/English instructor at California State University, Dominguez Hills. She is the managing editor of Red Hen Press, Granada Hills, California. She won the 1998 Allen Ginsberg Poetry Award. She wrote the libretto to the opera *Rio de Sangre*, which has been performed by the Los Angeles Master Chorale. She has written four books of poetry, a novel, one children's book, and she is the editor of four anthologies. She lives and writes in Los Angeles.

Lisha Adela Garcia is a bilingual, bicultural poet who has Mexico, the United States, and the land in between (Spanglish) in her work. She holds an M.F.A. from Vermont College. She is influenced by the American Southwest, the ghosts that haunt her labyrinth, and border culture. Garcia is a simultaneous interpreter and translator and most recently translated into English the Mexican poet Luis Armenta Malpica's book *The Will of Light*. She also has a Masters in International Management from Thunderbird School of Global Management. Her chapbook *This Stone Will Speak* has been published by Pudding House Press. Her poems have appeared in BestPoem.com, *Crab Orchard Review* and are forthcoming in anthologies from Eden River Press, Red Hen Press, and BlueLight Press. She currently resides in Arizona with Nube, her cat, and Chiquita, her dog.

Richard Garcia was born in San Francisco in 1941 to a Puerto Rican father and Mexican mother. His previous books of poetry include *The Persistence of Objects* (BOA Editions 2006), *Rancho Notorious* (BOA Editions 2001), and *The Flying Garcias* (University of Pittsburgh Press 1993). He holds an M.F.A. from the Warren Wilson Program for Writers. He has won many awards for his work, including a Pushcart Prize and fellowships from the National Endowment for the Arts, the California Arts Council, and the Cohen Award from *Ploughshares*. For 12 years he was Poet-in-Residence at Children's Hospital in Los Angeles, where he conducted poetry and art workshops for hospitalized children. He teaches in the Antioch University, Los Angeles, M.F.A. Low Residency Program and is on the teaching staff of the Idyllwild Poetry Festival. His poems have appeared in *The Georgia Review*, *Crazyhorse*, *Ploughshares*, and *Best American Poetry*. He lives with his wife Katherine Williams and their dog Louie on James Island, South Carolina, where he conducts private workshops at home and online. Of his poem in this anthology, "Maximum Security," he writes: "For me, poetry is the recovery of memory transformed through art."

Jane Gentry was born in Central Kentucky where she grew up on a farm at Athens. She now lives in Versailles. Her new book of poems *Portrait of the Artist as a White Pig* came out in 2006 from Louisiana State University Press, which also published her previous collection *A Garden in Kentucky* in 1995. An English professor at the University of Kentucky, she conducts poetry-writing workshops, teaches in the University Honors Program, and is advisor to *Jar*, a student-edited literary magazine. She has been awarded two Al Smith Fellowships by the Kentucky Arts council and has held fellowships at Yaddo in Saratoga Springs, New York, and at the Virginia Center for the Creative Arts at Lynchburg. She was appointed Kentucky Poet Laureate for 2007-2008.

Molly Gloss lives in Portland, Oregon. In 1996 she was the recipient of a prestigious Whiting Writers Award. Her novel *The Jump-Off Creek* (Houghton Mifflin 1989) is a Pacific Northwest classic, winner of the Oregon Book Award and the Pacific Northwest Booksellers Award, and a finalist for the PEN/Faulkner Award. *The Dazzle of Day* (Tor Books 1997), a novel of the near future, received the PEN West Fiction Prize and was a New York Times Notable Book. *Wild Life* (Simon and Schuster 2000), set in the woods and mountains of Washington State at the turn of the 20th century, won the James Tiptree Award. A new novel, *The Hearts of Horses*, was released November 2007 from Houghton Mifflin. Her first novel was a young adult fantasy/adventure, *Outside the Gates* (Atheneum 1986). Gloss's poem in this anthololgy, "Grief Moves out of the House," was written five years after the death of her husband Ed in February 2000, less than three months after being diagnosed with metastatic ocular melanoma. They were married 33 years. Of this poem, she writes, "Personifying grief as a lover came easily to me, but of course I couldn't have written the poem any sooner than I did."

William Greenway's ninth full-length collection, *Everywhere at Once*, is forthcoming from the University of Akron Press Poetry Series. Other collections include *Ascending Order* (University of Akron Press 2003), winner of the 2004 Ohioana Poetry Book of the Year Award, and *I Have My Own Song For It: Modern Poems of Ohio* (University of Akron Press 2002), which he co-edited with Elton Glaser, *Fishing at the End of the World* (Word Press 2005), and a chapbook, *Twice Removed* (Main Street Rag 2006). His poems have appeared in *Poetry, American Poetry Review, Georgia Review, Southern Review, Poetry Northwest, Shenandoah*, and *Prairie Schooner*. He has won the Helen and Laura Krout Memorial Poetry Award, the Larry Levis Editors' Prize from *Missouri Review*, the Open Voice Poetry Award from The Writer's Voice, the State Street Press Chapbook Competition, an Ohio Arts Council Grant, and was 1994 Georgia Author of the Year. He's Distinguished Professor of English at Youngstown State University. Of his poem "Eurydice," which has also been published in his new collection under the title "Persephone," Greenway writes: "The poem had two titles because I don't know yet if my wife will be lost to me for all time, after her stroke, or for just a season. Whatever myth you prefer, the experience has taught me to look neither backwards, nor too far into the future for fear of what I might see."

Rachel Eliza Griffiths is a Cave Canem fellow and received her M.F.A. from Sarah Lawrence College. Her poetry, fiction, and photography/art have appeared or are forthcoming in *Callaloo, Indiana Review, Puerto Del Sol, Saranac Review, Brilliant Corners*, and others. She lives in New York.

Barbara G. S. Hagerty is a poet, writer, and photographer who lives in Charleston, South Carolina. A graduate of The Writing Seminars at The Johns Hopkins University, she is the author of two non-fiction books as well as numerous essays, columns, and articles. She is currently working on a book of poems. Of her poem in this anthology, "Visiting Virginia P.," Hagerty writes: "Once upon a time, before entering a 12-step program in Atlanta, Virginia and I inhabited the same parallel universe of chaos and insanity. To meet, so many years later, her son—tall, healthy, born in her recovery phase and thus spared a mother's addiction-fueled craziness—was a palpable measurement of how far our heroines' journeys have taken us."

Donald Hall was born in New Haven, Connecticut, in 1928. He had his first work published at the age of 16. He earned a B.A. from Harvard in 1951 and a B. Litt. from Oxford in 1953. Donald Hall has published numerous books of poetry, most recently *White Apples and the Taste of Stone: Selected Poems 1946-2006* (Houghton Mifflin 2006), *The Painted Bed* (Houghton Mifflin 2002), and *Without: Poems* (Houghton Mifflin 1998), which was published on the third anniversary of the death of his wife, the poet Jane Kenyon, from leukemia. Other notable collections include *The One Day* (Ticknor & Fields 1988), which won the National Book Critics Circle Award, the *Los Angeles Times* Book Prize, and a Pulitzer Prize nomination; *The Happy Man* (Random House 1986), which won the Lenore Marshall Poetry Prize; and *Exiles and Marriages* (Viking Press 1955), which was the Academy of American Poetry's Lamont Poetry Selection for 1956. Besides poetry, Donald Hall has written books on baseball, the sculptor Henry Moore, and the poet Marianne Moore. He is also the author of children's books, including *Ox-Cart Man* (Viking Juvenile 1979), which won the Caldecott Medal; short stories, including *Willow Temple: New and Selected Stories* (Houghton Mifflin 2003); and plays. He has also published several autobiographical works, such as *The Best Day The Worst Day: Life with Jane Kenyon* (Houghton Mifflin 2005) and *Life Work* (Beacon Press 1993), which won the New England Book award for nonfiction. Hall has edited more than two dozen textbooks and anthologies. He served as poetry editor of *The Paris Review* from 1953 to 1962, and as a member of editorial board for poetry at Wesleyan University Press from 1958 to 1964. His honors include two Guggenheim fellowships, the Poetry Society of America's Robert Frost Silver medal, a Lifetime Achievement award from the New Hampshire Writers and Publisher Project, and the Ruth Lilly Prize for poetry. Hall also served as Poet Laureate of New Hampshire from 1984 to 1989. In June 2006, Hall was appointed the Library of Congress's fourteenth Poet Laureate Consultant in Poetry. He lives in Danbury, New Hampshire.

Thérése Halscheid's recent chapbook spans three decades of her work, published by Pudding House Publications under its *Greatest Hits* series. Other collections of poems are *Uncommon Geography* (Carpenter Gothic 2006), which was a Finalist Award for the Paterson Poetry Prize and *Without Home* (Kells 2001). She is a visiting writer in schools in the U.S. and has taught abroad in England and the Ural Mountains of Russia. Of her poem in this anthology, "Peasants Around Small Fires," she writes: "I had the chance to teach in Russia in a Russian/American exchange in the Fall of 1991, just before Communism collapsed in December. My position was in the Ural Mountains, the town of Nizhni Tagil, a city that Stalin had closed because it was the place of a Gulag. I was among the first group of Americans to re-enter since WWII. Here, peasants fished on the Volga River and picked mushrooms in the forest. At dusk, I could see small fires along the riverbanks, where they were cooking their fish. This was my first insight into peasantry and I was very moved. The teacher I lived with, as well as a photographer that I connected with, taught me about Kitchen Talks ... tiny kitchens where they would meet at night and share their beliefs. The photographer's work had been banned because he dared to expose the rebirth of spirituality. The church in town, the Church of St. Nicholas, had been used as a place to store ammunition during WWII, and the icons had been used for firewood. Still, the peasants managed to hide their personal icons and managed, through the Kitchen Talks, to secretly hold their religious beliefs. During the summer of 1993, I was asked to lead a group of American students through Russia from Moscow to St. Petersburg. We visited the Gold Ring Cities, five small cities, very old and spiritual. By this time, Communism had collapsed and a rebirth of religion was evident, churches were being reopened, and it was as if people were allowing themselves to openly express their belief in God, although, reticent and still somewhat afraid. We were rowing one dusk on the Volga River, and I saw the small fires from the peasants once more … small campfires along the banks of the river, saw that they had been cooking the fish they had caught that day, eating the mushrooms of the forest, and the berries. This time, I imagined their speech … based on what had been shared with me in the kitchens and villages. I moved those words to the riverbanks, around the fires along the Volga."

Farideh Hassanzadeh is an Iranian poet, translator, and freelance journalist who lives in Teheran. Her first book of poetry was published when she was twenty-two. Her poems appear in the anthologies *Contemporary Women Poets of Iran* and *Anthology of Best Women Poets*. She writes regularly for *Golestaneh*, *Iran News*, *Jamejam* and many literary magazines. Her poems, translated into English, have appeared in ezines like *Kritya*, *Jehat*, *interpoetry*, *Muse India*, *earthfamilyalpha* and *Thanalonline*. The first volume of her three-volume anthology of Contemporary American Poetry was published in 2007. She is the author of *Eternal Voices: Interviews with Poets East and West* and *The Last Night with Sylvia Plath: Essays on Poetry*. She has extensively translated world literature into Persian. Among her several translations are: *Selected Poems of T.S. Eliot*, *Anthology of Contemporary African Poetry* (edited by Gerald Moore and Uili Beier), and *Women Poets of the World*. In an interview with the magazine *Foreign Policy In Focus* on June 12, 2007, Hassanzadeh said this of her poem that appears in this anthology,

"I, I Who Have Nothing": "Before [the Iran-Iraq] war, my poetry was not familiar with words like: bombs, alarming sounds, ruins and fears. The sky and the beauty of clouds or the brightness of stars turned into a terrible roof above me where bombs could fall and explode all my dreams. Before war I used to see the killed only on TV, in the news about Palestine. I never was able to smell the warm stream of blood shown in massacre reports. War acted like a sleight of hand to make the distance between me and the world disappear, beyond the TV. It turned my first little son to a bird without wings to fly, a bird good only to be buried forever...My son, before he could experience the fear of his first day of school, experienced the fear of his last breath, his hands gone with the bombs. He never tasted the joy of putting a pencil on paper to write a word...How did I cope with the loss? Honestly I could forget his death but my feet, indifferent to me, sometimes go to the place where my son was bombed. All mothers of dead children know their children never leave them, never forget them. They wait for the night to return in dreams. They live behind the closed eyelids of their mothers."

Joy Harold Helsing lives in the Sierra Nevada foothills of Northern California. Her work has appeared most recently in *The Aurorean, Bellowing Ark, Brevities, California Quarterly, Centrifugal Eye, Leading Edge, The Lyric, Mobius, PKA's Advocate, Poetry Depth Quarterly, The Raintown Review,* and *Rattlesnake Review.* She has published three chapbooks and one collection, *Confessions of the Hare* (PWJ Publishing 2005). Of her poem in this anthology, "Turnabout," she writes, "The poem was inspired by my recollection of the frightening, infuriating time many years ago when I was struggling to break out of an abusive relationship."

Sister Lou Ella Hickman, I.W.B.S. has been a member of the Roman Catholic Sisters of the Incarnate Word and Blessed Sacrament since 1970. She has an undergraduate degree in elementary education and a master's in theology. She taught school for 17 years and served as a librarian part-time for ten years. She worked in a Catholic parish for two years as a coordinator for adult religious education. She has published 200 articles and 150 poems as well as co-authored a book, *Catechizing with Religious*

Symbols (Resource Publications 1997). At present, she is a free-lance writer and works part-time in religious retail.

Diane Holland is a painter/printmaker as well as a poet with an M.F.A. in Art from the University of Wisconsin-Madison and an M.F.A. in Poetry from Warren Wilson Program for Writers. Her first collection, *The Hand Stayed From Its Desire* won the 2006 Predator Press chapbook prize and was nominated by Eleanor Wilner for a Pushcart Prize. Recent work has also appeared in *Lumina* where the poem "How It Happens" won the 2006 poetry contest judged by Mark Doty, in *Gulf Stream Review* and in *Crab Orchard Review*, *Comstock Review*, *West Wind Review*, and *Laurel Review*. She was a recent finalist for the Ruth Stone Prize. She divides her time between Oregon and Alaska where she taught at the University of Alaska, Anchorage. Of her poem in this anthology, "At Baggage Claim," she writes: "It seems that our lives are in constant flux between times of great good fortune and productivity and times of drifting or loss. The great wheel turns, and loss comes. And yet it can as well be an opening to vision, both literal and figurative. While we try to prepare, to pack for our lives what we think we'll need, the unexpected awaits. We have only to attend with insight as well as our eyes."

Liu Hongbin was born in 1962 in Qingdoa, China. He worked as a clerk, teacher, and journalist in China and was frequently harassed and questioned by the police for his literary and political activities. Four of his poems were posted around Tiananmen Square in 1989 during the events leading up to the massacre of hundreds of demonstrators in the square by the Chinese Army on June 4, 1989. He fled to London in the same year. In 1992, he began writing a Ph.D. dissertation in literature at the University of London and has since worked as a freelance journalist, lecturer, and visiting research fellow. Attempts to return to China to see his mother resulted in expulsion in 1997 and detention in 2004. He is banned from returning. He is the author of two previous collections of poems, *Dove of the East* (hand printed in 1983 and circulated privately and secretly in China) and *An Iron Circle* (Calendar 1992).

Faye J. Hoops' poems and short stories have appeared in *Sand Hills Literary Magazine*, *Feelings Poetry Journal*, *Bereavement Magazine*, and have been anthologized in *On My Mind* (Georgia Writers' Inc. 1999), *Words of Wonder Anthology* (Anderie Poetry Press 1996), and throughout the 1990s, 2000, and 2007 in the annual anthology *The Reach of Song* (Georgia State Poetry Society). She lives in Augusta, Georgia, and she published her first poem in 1971. She won second place in the 1997 Porter Fleming Writing Competition, sponsored by the Greater Augusta Arts Council. Of her poem in this anthology, "Parade," she writes: "I had two sons, but in 1980, my youngest son died of cancer at age 23. I did not write for 10 years after my son died. The day I was planting bulbs and found the toy soldier, I thought about them playing in the sand pile. When I placed the toy soldier upright with the bulb, I thought of spring and the colors from the bulbs and that gave me a moment of peace. My husband of 52 years died five years ago, and I have finally learned to reach for good and humorous memories in writing about my son and husband. My faith in seeing them again and my good memories pick me up when I am down."

Randall Horton is a poet originally from Birmingham, Alabama, now living in Albany, New York. He was runner up in the Main Street Rag Book Award and his manuscript *The Definition of Place* (Main Street Rag 2006) was published in its Editor's Select Series. He is also the co-editor of *Fingernails Across the Chalkboard: Poetry and Prose on HIV/AIDS from the Black Diaspora* (Third World Press 2007). He is a Cave Canem Fellow. Of his poem in this anthology "Notes on a Prodigal Son #5," he writes: "My father has been as essential to my life as breathing. 'Notes from a Prodigal Son' is a series of poems written to my father about my isolation in prison. In writing these poems, I felt I was getting closer to a reconciliation with my father for having disappointed him. 'Notes from a Prodigal Son #5' seeks to reconcile my felonious actions by remembering what it was I was trying to escape in my youth. In essence, by recovering the past, I move closer to recovering the relationship with my father."

Joan Houlihan is the author of *Hand-Held Executions: Poems & Essays* (Del Sol Press 2003) and *The Mending Worm* (New Issues Poetry Press

2006), winner of the Green Rose Award. Her third collection, *The Us*, is forthcoming from Tupelo Press. She is editor-in-chief of *Perihelion* and staff reviewer for the *Contemporary Poetry Review*. Her series of essays on contemporary poetry is published under the title *Boston Comment*. Her work has appeared or is forthcoming in many journals and magazines, including *Boston Review*, *Harvard Review*, *The Gettysburg Review*, *Poetry International*, *Fulcrum*, *Passages North*, *Columbia: A Journal of Literature and Arts*, *Gulf Coast*, *Pleiades*, *VOLT* and is anthologized in the *Iowa Anthology of New American Poetries* (University of Iowa Press 2004) and *The Book of Irish-American Poetry, 18th Century to Present* (University of Notre Dame 2007). She is founder and director of the Concord Poetry Center and of the Colrain Poetry Manuscript Conferences. Of her poem in this anthology, "Devon's Treatment," Houlihan writes: "This poem deals with the experience of living in the hospital for many months to be with my 19-year-old son as he recovered from an accident. My husband and I watched him through a week-long coma, then re-learning how to move, speak, eat, walk and finally come home."

Betty Lynch Husted's poems have been published in *Windfall Jane's Stories III*, *The Pedestal Magazine*, and *Triplopia*. One of her poems was nominated for a Pushcart Prize. A chapbook, *After Fire*, was published by Pudding House Press in 2002. A memoir *Above the Clearwater: Living on Stolen Land* (Oregon State University Press 2004) was a finalist for the Oregon Book Award as well as the Women Writing the West's WILLA Award and the Idaho Award for creative nonfiction. She has received an Oregon Arts Commission Individual Artist Award (2007) to work on a second memoir, *A Life With Class: The Stories We Don't Tell*, and essays from this work have been published in *Prairie Schooner*, *Fourth Genre*, *Oregon Humanities*, *Silk Road*, and elsewhere. She was a 1994 Fishtrap Fellow. Of her poem in this anthology, "Salvage Anthropology," Husted writes: "This poem describes an event experienced by an Indian friend. How is she and how are other Indian people to recover? The cultural losses inflicted on them are so immense we can hardly comprehend them, and grief and cultural disruption sometimes lead to the same kind of self-inflicted losses many other people experience—

e.g. alcoholism and drug addiction, as well as poverty. The subject of this poem is struggling with her grief after a funeral, and struggling to understand her identity. She thinks about a naming ceremony for her young daughter, who wants to know her real name—names in this inland northwest Indian culture are conferred in a community spiritual ceremony involving a huge giveaway of gifts, which take a year to make. These names provide a way of carrying on the person/s who formerly had that name as well as a gateway into the afterlife for the person whose name it is now."

Major Jackson lives in South Burlington, Vermont, and teaches English at the University of Vermont. His poems have appeared in the *American Poetry Review*, *Callaloo*, *Grand Street*, *Triquarterly*, and *The New Yorker*, among other journals, and in the anthology *Gathering Ground* edited by Toi Derricote and Cornelius Eady (University of Michigan 2006). The recipient of a Whiting Writers' Award, Jackson is one of two U.S. poets to receive a Library of Congress Witter Bynner fellowship in 2003. He also has received fellowships from the Bread Loaf Writers' Conference, Cave Canem, Inc., Pew Fellowship in the Arts, and the Fine Arts Work Center in Provincetown. His first collection, *Leaving Saturn* (University of Georgia Press 2002), was a finalist for the National Book Critics Circle Award. One of his poems in this anthology, "Allegheny," was drawn from a chapter in his book *Hoops* (W. W. Norton 2006) entitled "Letter to Brooks," which begins "Dear Gwendolyn."

Liesl Jobson is a freelance bassoon player living in Johannesburg. She is a poetry editor for *Mad Hatters' Review* and her writing has appeared in *The Southern Review, The Rambler, The Mississippi Review (online), Per Contra, Snow*vigate, elimae, 3:AM* and *Literary Mama* and in numerous South African journals and anthologies. She won the 2005 People Opposing Women Abuse/Women's Writing Poetry Competition and the 2006 Faye Goldie Award from the South African Writers' Circle. She received a "highly commended" in the 2006 Commonwealth Short Story Competition, the 2005 Ernst van Heerden Award from the University of the Witwatersrand, and a 2007 Community Publishing Grant from the Centre for the Book, National Library of South Africa. Her anthology of flash fiction *100 Papers* was published by Botsotso in April 2008. Of her poem in this anthology, "Missive from Shakaland," Jobson writes: "The poem marked a turning point for me after a savage divorce, which had left me feeling trapped, as if in a schism between the horrors of the old South Africa and the terrors of the new. For months I felt like I was terminally ill and would never recover. My daughter's visit to the countryside of my own childhood facilitated my reconnection to healing memories, to gratitude, and to the possibility of hope."

Ilya Kaminsky was born in Odessa, Ukraine, in 1977. In 1993, his family was granted asylum by the American government and came to the U.S. *Dancing in Odessa* (Tupelo Press 2004), his first full length collection, received the Tupelo Press Dorset Prize, The Whiting Writer's Award, The Addison M. Metcalf Award in Literature from the American Academy of Arts and Letters, and the *ForeWord Magazine* Best Poetry Book of the Year Award. He has won the Ruth Lilly Fellowship from the Poetry Foundation, publisher of *Poetry* magazine, and has received numerous other awards and prizes. He received his B.A. from Georgetown University and subsequently became Writer in Residence at Phillips Exeter Academy and has taught at numerous literary centers. He teaches in the graduate writing program at San Diego State University. In late 1990s, he co-founded Poets For Peace, an organization which sponsors poetry readings in the U.S. and other nations with a goal of supporting such relief organizations as Doctors Without Borders and Survivors International. Kaminsky graduated from law school in 2004 and has also worked as a Law Clerk at the National Immigration Law Center, and more recently at Bay Area Legal Aid, helping impoverished and homeless in solving their legal difficulties. Kaminsky became deaf from a bout with the mumps at the age of 4, and he writes of his synesthesia: "When I lost my hearing, I began to see voices." He also writes poetry in his native Russian. He currently lives in Berkeley, California with his wife, Katie Farris.

Sándor Kányádi was born in 1929 into a Hungarian peasant family in Transylvania, Romania. He had his education and career as an editor within his native culture that also nourished his poetry. After an early start, he garnered every literary prize in Romania and Hungary, and in the last two decades his poetry has been appearing in most European languages.

Shirley Kaufman, translator of Meir Wieseltier's poetry in this anthology, is a prize-winning American-Israeli poet and translator who has published eight volumes of her own poems, most recently *Roots in the Air: New and Selected* (Copper Canyon Press 1996) and *Threshold* (Copper Canyon Press 2003). She has also published several books of translations, among them works by Amir Gilboa and Abba Kovner from Hebrew and by Judith Herzberg from Dutch.

Willie James King holds an M.F.A. in creative writing from the Queens University of Charlotte. His most recent collection, *The House in the Heart*, was published by Tebot Bach in 2007. He has two previous collections, *Wooden Windows* (SRLR Press 1999) and *At the Forest Edge* (Court Street Press 2005). He currently resides in Montgomery, Alabama.

Deborah Kolodji is the president of the Science Fiction Poetry Association and a member of the Haiku Society of America. She has published four chapbooks of poetry and her work has appeared in such diverse places as *Modern Haiku, Strange Horizons, Pearl, Poetpourri* (now *Comstock Review*), *Tales of the Unanticipated, The Mainichi Daily News, Frogpond, The Magazine of Speculative Poetry, Mythic Delirium, St. Anthony Messenger Magazine, Simply Haiku, Dreams and Nightmares, Scorched Earth*, and many others. She lives in Temple City, California.

Carolyn Kreiter-Foronda was appointed Poet Laureate, 2006-2008, for the Commonwealth of Virginia by Governor Timothy M. Kaine. She is the author of *Contrary Visions* (Scripta Humanistica 1988), *Gathering Light* (SCOP Publications, Inc. 1993), *Death Comes Riding* (SCOP Publications, Inc. 1999), *Greatest Hits, 1981-2000* (Puddinghouse Press 2001), and *River Country* (San Francisco Bay Press 2008), as well as co-editor of two poetry anthologies, *In a Certain Place* (SCOP Publications, Inc. 2000) and *Four Virginia Poets Laureate: A Teaching Guide* (The Poetry Society of Virginia 2006). Her poems have appeared in numerous publications, including *Nimrod, Cauteloso engaño del sentido, Prairie Schooner,*

Poet Lore, Mid-American Review, Antioch Review, Bay Splash, and *Passages North.* She holds a B.A. from the University of Mary Washington and two Master's degrees and a Ph.D. from George Mason University, where she received the university's first doctorate. In 2007 both universities gave her the Alumna of the Year Award. Her many poetry honors include three Pushcart Prize nominations, an Edgar Allan Poe First Place award, a finalist in "Discovery" *The Nation* poetry contest, a *Passages North* competition award, a *Spree* First Place award, and a *Phoebe* First Place award. She is also a visual artist, whose paintings have been widely displayed in galleries, nursing homes, and educational settings. She lives in the Tidewater region of Virginia with her husband, Patricio. Of her poem in this anthology, "Mother," she writes: "During the summer of my 16th year, I suffered an illness that left me so close to death that I recall rising out of my body and staring down on my own lifeless shape. By chance, our family doctor stopped by our house to check on me. Realizing the severity of my condition, he ordered that I be transported immediately to the hospital. After this close call, my senses sharpened and I began to receive messages from 'the other side.' Often these messages came from my mother in dreams. In this poem, I rely on the symbolic implications of 'moon' and 'stone' to suggest the permanency of her influence as a spiritual guide. One enduring lesson has been to make the most of the additional years I've been granted."

Kurtis Lamkin is a poet who plays the Kora, a beautiful 21-string West African instrument. He has performed his work internationally at festivals, concert halls, prisons, and universities. His poetry has been featured in several publications, including *Patterson Literary Review*, *Crazy Horse*, *Black American Literature Forum*, and *Elements of Literature*. Lamkin has performed on several radio and television shows and was one of the featured poets on Bill Moyers' "Fooling With Words" television special. His animated poetry "The Foxes Manifesto" was aired for two years on PBS. He has produced four CDs: *El Shabazz*, *Queen of Carolina*, *Magic Yams*, and *String Massage*. He has recently been inducted into the South Carolina Poetry Archives at Furman University, Greenville.

Stellasue Lee's book *Crossing the Double Yellow Line* (Bombshelter Press 2000) was nominated for a Pulitzer Prize. She received her Ph.D. from Honolulu University. Editor Emeritus at *Rattle*, she serves presently on the editorial board at Curbstone Press. She was born in the year of the dragon.

Jeffrey Levine is the founder, publisher, and editor-in-chief of Tupelo Press. He has won the Transcontinental Poetry Award, as well as the Larry Levis Poetry award, the *Mississippi Review* Poetry prize, the *Kestral* Poetry Prize, and the New Jersey Skyland Writers and Artists Association Award. Levine was a corporate lawyer in New York City and a professional musician in 1999 when he launched Tupelo Press, a small publishing house in Dorset, Vermont. He is a graduate of the University of Albany, State University of New York, where he majored in music and English. He then taught at Skidmore College, played with the Albany Symphony Orchestra and became a member of the Buffalo Philharmonic. He attended the Buffalo School of Law (State University of New York) and worked briefly as a criminal defense lawyer. He went on to spend 25 years in corporate law while continuing his work as a musician. His collections of poetry include *Mortal, Everlasting* (Pavement Saw Press 2002) and *Rumor of Cortez* (Red Hen Press 2005). His poems have appeared in *Barrow Street*, *5 AM*, *Beloit Poetry Journal*, *Alembic*, *Notre Dame Review*, *Yankee Magazine*, *New Orleans Review*, and other journals. He lives in West Harford, Connecticut.

Nancy Tupper Ling is the winner of the 2007 Pat Parnell Poetry Prize awarded by Chester College of New England as well as the 2005 Writer's Digest Grand Prize. Her chapbook of poetry is *Character* (Poet's Corner Press 2007) and her children's picture book is *My Sister, Alicia May* (Pleasant St. Press 2008). Other publication credits include: *Louisville Review*, *Potomac Review*, and *SLAB*. Of her poem in this anthology, "Another New England Winter," Tupper Ling writes, "Darkness is more than just seasonal in this poem. It is the place of sterility and extreme loneliness—a place from which an infertile couple emerges after their struggle to conceive. Ironically, it is only when the narrator surrenders to a High Power, lets go of everything that's beyond her control, that true recovery and Spring can begin."

Roseann Lloyd's most recent poetry collection is *Because of the Light* (Holy Cow! Press 2003). Her previous poetry collection, *War Baby Express* (Holy Cow! Press 1996)* received the Minnesota Book Award for Poetry in 1997. Her first collection of poetry *Tap Dancing for Big Mom* won the New rivers Minnesota Voices Contest in 1985. The anthology she co-edited, *Looking for Home: Women Writing About Exile* (Milkweed Editions 1990) was awarded the American Book Award in 1991. Her co-translation of the contemporary Norwegian novel *The House With the Blind Glass Windows*, written by Herbjørg Wassmo, was published by Seal Press in 1995. A community activist, Lloyd has taught writing classes at the Sexual Violence Center for survivors of sexual abuse. She is one of the founding members of the Silent Witnesses, a traveling memorial to women murdered by spouses, partners, or acquaintances in Minnesota in 1991, which has been replicated around the world.

Tom Lombardo is the editor of this anthology. He earned a B.S. from Carnegie-Mellon University, an M.S. from Ohio University, and an M.F.A. from Queens University of Charlotte. His poems have appeared in many journals in the U.S., the U.K., Canada, and India, including *Southern Poetry Review*, *Subtropics, Ambit*, *Hampden-Sydney Poetry Review*, *New York Quarterly*, *Kritya: A Journal for Our Time*, *Orbis*, *Salamander*, *Ars Medica*, *Pearl*, *Asheville Poetry Review,* and others. His criticism has been published in *New Letters*, *North Carolina Literary Review*, and *South Carolina Review*. His essays and other nonfiction have appeared in *Chrysalis Reader*, *IEEE Spectrum*, *Leisure* magazine, and other publications. He has taught courses in Aesthetics and in Creative Writing at the Atlanta College of Art. He was the founding editor-in-chief of WebMD, the world's most widely used health web site, and he lives in Midtown Atlanta, where he works as a freelance medical editor. Of his poem in this anthology, "Brother Christopher's Boys," he says, "For me, the poem unlocks the door to that mysterious year with Brother Christopher."

Naomi Ruth Lowinsky has been published in such literary journals as *Tiferat*, *Paterson Literary Review*, *Comstock Review*, and *Backwards City Review*. Her poems have been nominated for Pushcart Prizes three times. Her second collection of poems, *crimes of the dreamer*, was published in 2007 by Scarlet Tanager Books. She is a Jungian analyst in private practice in Berkeley, California, and the Poetry Editor of *Psychological Perspectives*.

Thomas Lux holds the Margaret T. and Henry C. Bourne Chair in Poetry at The Georgia Institute of Technology, Atlanta. In addition to having been on the writing faculties of the country's most prestigious M.F.A. and Creative Writing Programs (Columbia University, Boston University, University of Iowa, University of Michigan, University of Houston, and the University of California, Irvine, among others), Thomas Lux taught at Sarah Lawrence College for twenty-seven years, the last nineteen of which, he was director of its M.F.A. Program in Poetry. Lux has published ten books of poems, most recently *The Cradle Place* (Houghton Mifflin 2004), and seven Limited Edition books that have earned him, among other awards and prizes, the $100,000 Kingsley Tufts Poetry Prize, four Pushcart Prizes, and grants from the Mellon Foundation, the Guggenheim Memorial Foundation, and three from the National Endowment for the Arts. He has been further honored with the Bank of New York Award for Excellence in Teaching. In 2003, Lux was awarded an Honorary Doctorate of Letters from Emerson College, Boston.

Ed Madden is an associate professor of English at the University of South Carolina. His first book *Signals* (University of South Carolina Press 2008) was selected by Afaa Michael Weaver for the South Carolina Poetry Book Prize. His poems have been published or are forthcoming in *Solo*, *Los Angeles Review*, *River City*, *Southern Humanities Review*, *Arkansas Review*, and other journals. His work has also been included in *The Book of Irish American Poetry: From the Eighteenth Century to the Present* (Notre Dame 2007), *Southern Poetry Anthology: South Carolina* (*Texas Review* Press 2007), *Best New Poets 2007* (Samovar 2007), *A Millennial Sampler of South Carolina Poetry* (Ninety-Six Press 2005), and the collection *Gents, Bad Boys and Barbarians: New Gay Male Poetry* (Alyson 1994). Of his poem in this anthology, "Weekend," he writes: "Things that can't be fixed, things we want to fix, some hope, some acclimation, some acceptance."

Nicholas Mazza, Ph.D., is the founding and current editor of the *Journal of Poetry Therapy*, and author of *Poetry Therapy: Theory and Practice* (Brunner-Routledge 2003). Dr. Mazza is the Patricia V. Vance Professor of Social Work at the Florida State University College of Social Work, Tallahassee, Florida. He was co-editor of *Death and Trauma: The Traumatology of Grieving* (Taylor & Francis 1997). He holds Florida licenses in clinical social work, marriage and family therapy, and psychology. In addition to poetry therapy, his research interests include expressive writing and health, death and loss, arts and community practice, family and group counseling, and crisis intervention.

John McAllister is the author of a novel, *Line of Flight* (Bluechrome 2006) and a short story collection *The Fly Pool* (Black Mountain Press 2003). He is currently the facilitator of writing classes for Counties Meath and Cavan's Arts Councils (Ireland). He has an M.Phil. in Creative Writing from Trinity College, Dublin. Of his poem in this anthology, "Dog Days," he writes: "My father died when I was nine. He had been in hospital for two years before that so I have only the vaguest memories of him. I only remember love in the house, never him and my mother fighting. But they must have fought because he had the McAllister temper - a quick burst and then forgotten - and she had red hair. My mother was very reticent about her inner life but she did tell two stories of her early married life which I incorporated into 'Dog Days'. I'm only sorry that she died before I could write it."

Rebecca McClanahan is the author of nine books, most recently *Deep Light: New and Selected Poems* 1987-2007 (Iris Press 2007) and *The Riddle Song and Other Rememberings* (University of Georgia Press 2002), which won the Glasgow Prize in Nonfiction, and *Word Painting: A Guide to Writing More Descriptively* (Writer's Digest Books 2000). Her poems, essays, and stories have appeared in *Ms. Magazine, The Georgia Review, The Gettysburg Review, Southern Review, Kenyon Review, Boulevard, Seventeen,* and numerous literary magazines and anthologies throughout the U.S. McClanahan has received a Pushcart Prize in fiction, the Wood Prize from *Poetry* magazine, and the Carter prize for her essay in *Shenandoah*. Her work appears in *The Best American Essays 2001, The Best American Poetry 1998,* and has been aired on

NPR's "The Writer's Almanac," "The Sound of Writing," and "Living on Earth." McClanahan, who earned a Ph.D. and M.A.T. from the University of South Carolina and a B.A. from California State University, currently teaches in the M.F.A. program of Queens University of Charlotte, the *Kenyon Review* Writers' Workshop, and the Hudson Valley Writers' Center. Before moving to New York in 1998, she co-directed The University of North Carolina Writing Project and its affiliates, the Open Institute and the Reading-Writing Institute. For fifteen years she was Writer-in-Residence/Director of the Charlotte-Mecklenburg Poetry-in-the-Schools Program, for which she received a Governor's Award of Excellence.

Jim McGarrah serves as poetry editor for *Southern Indiana Review*. His memoir *A Temporary Sort of Peace*, which reflects his experiences as a combat Marine in Vietnam, was released by Indiana Historical Society Press in 2008. His first book of poems *Running the Voodoo Down* (Elixir Press 2003), won the Elixir Press Editor's Choice Award. His poems, essays, and stories have appeared in many literary magazines, including most recently in *Under the Sun*, *Café Review*, *Connecticut Review*, *Cedar Hill Review*, *Elixir*, *Unbound Magazine*, and *North American Review*. He has been nominated for a Pushcart Prize and a finalist twice for the James Hearst Poetry Contest. McGarrah holds an M.F.A. in writing from Vermont College and an M.A. in Liberal Studies from the University of Southern Indiana. Of his poem in this anthology, "Peace," McGarrah writes: "I wrote this poem for a return trip to Vietnam in 2005 as part of a ceremony conducted by the Ministry of Art and Literature in Hue. One of their national poets, Vo Que, and I exchanged poems as a token of mutual respect, and read them aloud for the audience. It helped bring about a sense of closure for me on that era of my life."

Jenni Meredith is a journalist and poet. She has two collections of poems; *Snow Ewes Crowing Over Split Snails* (Pocket Books 1991) and *You're Really Cutting Me Up?* (Cathap 2001) and her writing has been published in anthologies such as *Bigger than the Sky* (Women's Press 1999), *Mustn't Grumble* (Women's Press 1994), *The Bees Sneeze* (Stride 1992), *Under the Asylum Tree* (Survivors Poetry 1995), *Speaking Our Minds* (Macmillan / OUP

1996), *La Faccia Scura Della Luna* (Turin 1998), *Authors & Artists, Introduction Series 7* (Windows Publications, Eire, 2007), and *Tenth Annual Suruga Baika Literary Festival, Selected Works*; (Daichu-ji Temple, Shizuoka-ken, Japan 2008). Her animated poetry video *Through the Pane*, funded by an Arts Council of England grant, has been screened in Europe, Africa, and the Middle East and won an award in Turin's Noi Gli Altri festival. Another poetry video, *Shifting Shadows*, has been screened in Helsinki's Kynniskino, where it won a festival award, and in many other cities throughout Europe, North America, India and the Middle East. Her poetry soundscapes and performance tracks have been podcast on Artwave Radio (Greece), Dover Street Podcast Radio, (U.K.), NDAF podcast (U.K.), and G1 Podcast (U.S.). She lives in North Essex, England, where she collaborates with her husband, Tony, on animated videos, web art, and ceramics. Of her poem in this anthology, "Vertical Blinds," she writes: "When writing about overcoming distress, I thought about the things which had helped me through dark times in the past. I think focusing on 'Now', living for the present, not the past or the future, can alleviate stress. It certainly helped me. So I tried to encapsulate that in this poem. It is about setting yourself achievable goals, about climbing the mountain one step at a time. And when things begin to build up and get on top of me, I think about the slits of sun struggling through Venetian blinds and mentally force the plastic strips apart to let the rays grow stronger and wider to illuminate my clouds."

Susan Meyers is the author of *Keep and Give Away* (University of South Carolina Press 2006), which was the winner of the South Carolina Poetry Book Prize, the 2007 Southern Independent Booksellers Alliance Book Award for Poetry, and the Brockman-Campbell Book Award. Her chapbook *Lessons in Leaving* received the 1998 Persephone Press Book Award. A long-time writing instructor, she has an M.F.A. from Queens University of Charlotte. She lives with her husband in the rural community of Givhans, South Carolina. Of her poem in this anthology, "That Year," Meyers writes: "It was written when I looked back and realized that grief over my mother's impending death had managed to surface in its own way, even though I had tried to pretend to myself that I was fully in control of my emotions. What relief, I remember, planting all those pansies and bulbs."

Joseph Mills holds degrees in literature form the University of Chicago, the University of New Mexico, and the University of California-Davis. He is currently a faculty member of the North Carolina School of the Arts in Winston-Salem, where he teaches English and humanities. His poetry has appeared in numerous journals and magazines. His newest collection of poems, *Angels, Thieves, and Winemakers*, was released in 2008 by Press 53, Winston-Salem, North Carolina, and he recently edited a collection of film essays *A Hundred Years of the Marx Brothers* for Cambridge Scholars Publishing. Of his poem in this anthology, "Recipes," he writes: "We all know that diet affects physical health, but I believe that food affects our mental health, and, more specifically, the way we prepare our food can both indicate our current state-of-mind and affect it. Cooking can be an exercise in focusing ourselves."

Barbara Mitchell has won numerous poetry contests and her poetry has been widely published. She is the creator of a multi-media presentation featuring her poetry and is frequently called to judge poetry contests. She also leads creative writing workshops. She lives in Edmonton, Alberta, Canada. Of her poem in this anthology, "The Boy of Silence," she writes: "The key to recovery in this poem is the father's final acceptance of his son's autistic condition. In learning from his son's silence, the silence becomes a communion. The boy receives the warmth and acceptance of his father, even while the father is learning acceptance." Of her poem "Small Courage," she writes: "The recovery is in the consciousness of the narrator's own small voice reaching her in a crucial moment. This woman suggested to me that it was at that exact point in her abusive cycle with this man that she decided, chose, determined, struggled, winced but boldly met up with her lost voice and the voice, in turn, fueled her beginning to a recovery by leaving the abusive situation. "

Majid Naficy fled Iran in 1983 a year and a half after the execution of his wife Ezzat Tabaian, January 7, 1982, in Evin prison in Tehran. His brother Sa'id and his brother-in-law Hossein were also executed. He has published two collections of poetry, *Muddy Shoes* (Beyond Baroque Books 1999) and *Father and Son* (Red Hen Press 2003) as well as his doctoral dissertation, "Modernism and Ideology in Persian Literature" (University Press of America). His poetry has been anthologized in *Poets Against War* edited by Sam Hamill (Nation Books 2003) and *Strange Times, My Dear: The Pen Anthology of Contemporary Iranian Literature*" edited by N. Mozaffari and A. Karimi (Arcade Publishing 2005). He is the co-editor of the literary journal of Iranian Writers' Association in Exile and the author of more than twenty books in Persian. He lives in Los Angeles.

Aimee Nezhukumatathil was born in Chicago, Illinois in 1974. She received her B.A. in English and received her M.F.A. in poetry and creative non-fiction from The Ohio State University. Her first full-length collection of poems *Miracle Fruit* won the 2003 Judge's Prize in Poetry from Tupelo Press, Dorset, Vermont, and was published by Tupelo. Her most recent collection is *At the Drive-in Volcano* (Tupelo Press 2007). She is the author of a chapbook, *Fishbone* (Snail's Pace Productions 2000), and was the Middlebrook Poetry Fellow at the Institute of Creative Writing at the University of Wisconsin. She is currently an assistant professor of English at the State University of New York, Fredonia.

Valerie Nieman is the author of a poetry collection *Wake Wake Wake* (Press 53 2006). Her poetry was earlier collected in two chapbooks and has appeared in journals such as *Blackbird, Poetry, New Letters, REDiViDER*, and *West Branch*, and in numerous anthologies. She is the author of a collection of short fiction, *Fidelities* (West Virginia University Press 2004) and two novels, *Survivors* (Van Neste Books 2000) and *Neena Gathering* (Haynes Publications 1988). A former newspaper reporter and editor, she continues to produce travel writing for major newspapers. She has received an NEA creative writing fellowship in poetry, two Elizabeth Simpson Smith prizes in fiction, and the Greg Grummer Prize in poetry. She received an M.F.A. from Queens University of Charlotte and now teaches writing at North Carolina A&T State University.

Tolu Ogunlesi was born in 1982. He is the author of a collection of poetry *Listen to the Geckos Singing From a Balcony* (Bewrite Books 2004). His fiction and poetry have appeared in *Wasafiri, The Obituary Tango* (Caine Prize

Anthology 2006), *Sable*, *Orbis*, *Eclectica*, and elsewhere, and are forthcoming in *Tipton Poetry Journal* and *Jelly Paint*. In 2007 he won a Dorothy Sargent Rosenberg poetry prize. He currently lives in Lagos, Nigeria.

Gail Peck is a graduate of the M.F.A. program for writers at Warren Wilson College. Her chapbooks include *New River* (North Carolina Writers' Network 1993), which won the North Carolina Harperprints Award, *Foreshadow* (Main Street Rag 2002), and *From Terezin* (Pudding House 2008), which comprises 20 poems based on the artwork of the children who were interned at Terezin Concentration Camp during World War II. Her full-length collections include *Drop Zone* (*Texas Review* Press 1994), which won the *Texas Review* Breakthrough Contest, and *Thirst* (Main Street Rag 2004). Her poems and essays have appeared in *The Southern Review*, *Greensboro Review*, *Louisville Review*, *Cimarron Review*, *Mississippi Review*, *Rattle*, *Southern Poetry Review*, *Kestrel*, *Brevity*, and elsewhere. Her work has been widely anthologized, and she was a 2007 finalist for the *Nimrod/Hardman* Award. Of her poem in this anthology, "I'll Never," Peck writes: "I had been dealing with my sister's alcoholism for many years, and the circumstances of her death were as out of my control as my inability to help her with her addiction. That day when the unexpected snowflakes fell I knew I was reaching some acceptance. Nature was offering solace unattainable to me through my own will."

J. E. Pitts is a writer and visual artist. His poems, essays, and illustrations have appeard in many magazines and literary journals. A graduate of the University of Mississippi, he is the poetry editor of *Oxford American*, co-founded and co-edits the experimental literary journal *VOX*, and lives in Oxford, Mississippi. He was awarded a literary fellowship in poetry from the Mississippi Arts Commission in 2006. *The Weather of Dreams* (David Robert Books 2007), from which his poem "Scar Inventory" was drawn for this anthology, is his first collection of poetry.

Iain Haley Pollock lives in Philadelphia and teaches English at Chestnut Hill Academy. He received an M.F.A. in Creative Writing from Syracuse University and is a member of the Cave Canem Workshop for African

American poets. His work has appeared or is forthcoming in *Boston Review*, *Callaloo,* and *Crab Orchard Review.*

Barbara Presnell's collection, *Piece Work*, won the 2006 Cleveland State University Poetry Center's First Book Prize, and was published by CSU in 2007. A portion of the poems was awarded the 2004 Linda Flowers Prize from the North Carolina Humanities Council and was published as *Sherry's Prayer*, as part of the *North Carolina Crossroads* series. In addition, she has published three chapbooks: *Snake Dreams*, which won the Zoe Kincaid Brockman Award from the North Carolina Poetry Society; *Unravelings*, which won the Longleaf Press Award and the Oscar Arnold Young Award from the North Carolina Poetry Council; and *Los Hijos*, set in Galeana, Nuevo Leon, Mexico. Her poems have appeared in *The Southern Review, Cimarron Review, Laurel Review, North Carolina Literary Review, Tar River Poetry*, and other journals, and in the anthologies, *Listen Here: Women Writing in Appalachia* (University of Kentucky 2004) and *Claiming the Spirit Within: A Sourcebook of Women's Poetry* (Beacon 1996). She's a native of Asheboro, North Carolina, holds the M.F.A. in Creative Writing from the University of North Carolina-Greensboro, lives in Lexington, North Carolina, with her husband and son, and teaches at the University of North Carolina-Charlotte. Of her poem in this anthology, she says: "I wrote 'Where They Come From, Where They Go' when I was teaching poetry to pregnant girls at the Florence Crittendon Home in Kentucky. The girl in the poem represents not just the girl who ran away but all the girls there and so many more like them. For Tina, recovery is only hope, as vague and uncertain as the dark night she wanders."

Anna Rabinowitz's most recent collection of poetry was highly acclaimed *The Wanton Sublime* (Tupelo Press 2006), an extended meditation upon the experiences of the Roman Catholic icon, the Virgin Mary, from the Annunciation by an angel of her conception of Jesus through his ultimate Crucifixion, in which the author cuts through the traditional baggage of piety and myth to expose the essential humanity of Mary, and ultimately, all women. Her other volumes of poetry were *At the Site of Inside Out* (University of Massachusetts Press 1997), which won the

Juniper Prize, and *Darkling: A Poem* (Tupelo Press 2001), which has been produced as an experimental multi-media music theatre work by American Opera Projects. Other honors include a National Endowment for the Arts Fellowship. She lives in New York City where she is Publisher and Executive Editor of *American Letters and Commentary*.

Ron Rash's family has lived in the southern Appalachian Mountains since the mid-1700's, and this region is the primary focus of his writing. Rash grew up in Boiling Springs, North Carolina, and graduated from Gardner-Webb College and Clemson University. In 1994 he was awarded an NEA Poetry Fellowship and won the Sherwood Anderson Prize in 1996. In 2001 he won the Novello Festival Novel Award and in 2002 was awarded *ForeWord Magazine's* Gold Medal in Literary Fiction for his novel *One Foot in Eden* (Novello Festival Press 2002). The novel was also named Appalachian Book of the Year. His second novel, *Saints in the River* (Henry Holt 2004) was named Best Fiction Book of the Year by Southern Independent Booksellers Alliance and the Southern Book Critics Circle. In 2005 he won an O. Henry award for his story "Speckled Trout," which appeared in his collection of stories *Chemistry and Other Stories* (Picador 2007). His poetry and fiction have appeared in over one hundred journals, magazines, and anthologies, including *The Longman Anthology of Southern Literature*, *Oxford American*, *Sewanee Review*, *Yale Review*, *Kenyon Review*, *New England Review*, *Southern Review*, *Shenandoah* and *Poetry*. His other books include three volumes of poetry and three collections of stories. His third novel, *The World Made Straight* (Henry Holt 2006) won a Sir Walter Raleigh Award. In March of 2005 he was given the James Still Award by the Fellowship of Southern Writers. His fourth novel, *Serena*, is forthcoming from Harper Collins.

J. Stephen Rhodes served as the academic dean of Memphis Theological Seminary and as a Presbyterian pastor prior to taking up writing full time. His poetry has appeared in *Shenandoah, Tar River Poetry, The William and Mary Review, Kennesaw Review*, and *The International Poetry Review*. He is currently working on a book dealing with the relationship between service and self-care and is seeking publication of his first book of poetry. He lives with his wife, Ann, on a farm in south central Kentucky. Of his poem in this anthology, "This New Never," he writes: "I wrote this poem two months after my daughter's suicide. She was halfway through her senior year of college when she died. This poem helped me grieve and give voice to a complex array of feelings. Perhaps, as much as anything, the poem names and sings about Rebecca's and my deep kinship, even in the midst of some alienation between the two of us—a kinship I have come to celebrate more since I wrote the poem."

Alexa Selph, a native Atlantan, has an M.A. in English from Georgia State University. She has worked for many years as a freelance book editor, and since 2001, she has taught classes in poetry at the Emory Center for Lifelong Learning. Her poems have been published in *Poetry, Habersham Review, Modern Haiku, Georgia State University Review, Connecticut Review,* and *Blue Mesa Review.* Of her poem in this anthology, "Therapy," she writes: "Some years ago I found myself, rather inexplicably, in a dark place emotionally. A few sessions with a therapist helped me enormously, and I came to see the experience as analogous to a kind of evolution, which is reflected in the extended metaphor of the poem." Of her poem "Leavings" she writes: "Relationships are endlessly fascinating to me, especially the way that hurt and anger can transform themselves over time into a kind of benevolent acknowledgment of what was good in the relationship, much the same way that discarded food can ultimately become something nourishing and even beautiful."

Deema K. Shehabi was born in Kuwait in 1970 to Palestinian parents. Her poems have appeared in *The Atlanta Review, Bat City Review, Crab Orchard, DMQ Review, Drunken Boat, Flyway, The Kenyon Review, Literary Imagination, The Mississippi Review, Siecle 21* (France), *Valparaiso Poetry Review,* and *The Jordan Times.* Her poems have been anthologized in *The Poetry of Arab Women* (Interlink Books 2001), *The Space Between Our Footstep,: Poems from the Middle East* (Simon and Schuster 1998), *Inclined to Speak: Contemporary Arab-American Poetry* (University of Arkansas Press 2008), *The Body Eclectic (Henry Holt and Company 2002)* and *Arab-American and Diaspora Literature* (Interlink Books, forthcoming). She is currently Vice-President for the Radius of Arab-American Writers and resides in

Northern California with her husband and two sons. Of her poem in this anthology, "At the Dome of the Rock," she writes: "The seed of the poem began on a visit to Jerusalem many winters ago. When you go to Jerusalem, you feel two things simultaneously: ecstatic, surreal lightness and the extreme weight of history. I was watching an old lady praying at the mosque, and even though she seemed very sad, she was also quite rooted in her surroundings. I realized how that very rootedness helped her recover from the daily struggles of life. In that rootedness, I discovered her power to overcome."

Kevin Simmonds is a writer and musician originally from New Orleans. His writing has appeared in the journals *Callaloo*, *FIELD*, *Massachusetts Review*, *Poetry*, and *Salt Hill* and in the anthologies *The Ringing Ear: Black Poets Lean South* (University of Georgia 2007) and *Gathering Ground* edited by Toi Derricote and Cornelius Eady (University of Michigan 2006). He wrote the music for *Wisteria: Twilight Songs of the Swamp Country* and *Hope*, both featuring the poetry of Kwame Dawes. He has received fellowships from Cave Canem, the Atlantic Center for the Arts and the Fulbright Program. He teaches and writes in San Francisco.

Marcia Slatkin, a former English teacher, now plays cello, takes photographs, and writes. Her first collection of poems *A Season's Milking* (Pudding House Press 2003) uses life in a backyard barnyard as metaphor for human conflict and closeness. Her chapbook *A Late Blessing* (Finishing Line Press 2005) examines the mother-daughter relationship as mother declines and daughter becomes caregiver. Her fiction won two PEN awards and has been published widely. Sixteen of her one-act plays have been produced in New York City, San Diego, and Long Island, New York. Honors include Samuel French finals. Her children are grown and she lives in Shoreham, Long Island, with her partner, Dan. Of her poem in this anthology, "A Late Blessing," she writes: "From her 86th to her 90th year my mother lived with me, in the decline of Alzheimer's Disease, and depended on me to manage a complex vitamin and medicine regimen as well as activities of daily living that she could no longer attend to. 'A Late Blessing' deals with *my recovery* of a loving relationship which had not existed since early childhood. I discovered that beneath her fiercely judgmental and controlling facade there was humor, warmth, gratitude, affection. The anger and pain that I carried melted away. During the four years that she lived with me, I was healed. She is now in a home in Denver, Colorado, near my sister, who superintends her care. She is doing as well as people can do in such facilities."

Paul Sohar got to pursue his life-long interest in literature full-time when he went on disability from his job in a chemistry lab. The results have slowly crept into *Chiron, Grain, Kenyon Review, Main Street Rag, New Delta Review, Poem, Poesy, Poetry Motel, Rattle,* and seven books of translations from the Hungarian, from which were drawn the two poems in this anthology by Sándor Kányádi and György Faludy, and most recently a volume of his own poetry, *Homing Poems* (Iniquity Press 2005).

Satyendra Srivastava was born in Azamgarh, Uttar Pradesh, India. He studied at the University of Poona from 1953-57, and the University of London from 1962-77, receiving his Ph.D. in history in 1978. He lectured in Indian Studies at the University of Toronto from 1968-71 and at the University of Cambridge from 1980-2003. With many published collections of poetry in Hindi, as well as plays for the stage and radio, he has also been a columnist for various Indian Publications. He writes in both Hindi and English. He has traveled widely to read his poems: from the U.S., Japan, and Russia to South Africa, Israel, and Egypt, among many other nations. His collections of poetry published in English are *Talking Sanskrit to Fallen Leaves* (Peepal Tree Press 1995), *Between Thoughts* (Samvad 1998), *Another Silence* (Samvad 2003), and *Sir Winston Churchill Knew My Mother* (Ambit Books 2006) from which the poems in this anthology have been reprinted. He has received several awards for his writing. He lives in London and Cambridge and frequently travels back to India.

William Stafford was born in Hutchinson, Kansas, in 1914. He received a B.A. and an M.A. from the University of Kansas at Lawrence and, in 1954, a Ph.D. from the University of Iowa. During the Second World War, Stafford was a conscientious objector and worked in the civilian public service camps—an experience he recorded in the prose memoir *Down My Heart* (1947). He married Dorothy Hope Frantz in 1944; they had four children. In 1948 Stafford moved to Oregon to teach at Lewis and Clark College. Though he traveled and read his work widely, he taught at Lewis and Clark until his retirement in 1980. His first major collection of poems, *Traveling Through the Dark* (Harper & Row 1963), was published when Stafford was 48 years old and has been re-issued. It won the National Book Award in 1963. He went on to publish more than sixty-five volumes of poetry and prose. Among his many honors and awards were a Shelley Memorial Award, a Guggenheim Fellowship, and a Western States Lifetime Achievement Award in Poetry. In 1970, he was the Consultant in Poetry to the Library of Congress (a position currently known as the Poet Laureate). Among his best-known books are *The Rescued Year* (Harper & Row 1966), *Stories That Could Be True: New and Collected Poems* (Harper & Row 1977), *Writing the Australian Crawl: Views on the Writer's Vocation* (University of Michigan Press 1978), and *The Darkness Around Us Is Deep: Selected Poems* (Harper Perennial 1997). William Stafford died at his home in Lake Oswego, Oregon, on August 28, 1993.

Dennis Ward Stiles was raised on a small farm in northern Illinois. He graduated from the U.S. Air Force Academy in 1964, and spent thirty years in the Air Force as a pilot and military diplomat. His work has appeared in many distinguished journals and anthologies. Pudding House published his fifth poetry chapbook, *Humdinger,* in 2007. He has been president of The Poetry Society of South Carolina twice, and served one term as Poet in Residence at the Gibbes Museum of Art. He lives in Charleston, South Carolina, with his wife Mary Jane, and co-owns America by Foot, Inc., a national walking-tour company. Of his poem in this anthology, "Bringing You Back," he writes: "After common sense prevailed and a love affair ended, I was heartsick but healing. The poem helped me define my state of mind, and to celebrate my lover and my lingering feelings for her from a new distance. Years have gone by, but the poem still keeps me in touch with a particularly beautiful time in my life. The pain of losing what we had has never really disappeared, but has turned into an almost-pleasant ache."

C. C. Thomas has been published in *The Chaffin Journal, Hot Metal Press, The Litchfield Review, Bellowing Ark, Toasted Cheese, Taj Mahal Review* and *Bibliophilos* among others, and has appeared as a featured poet at The Kentucky Folk Art Center in Morehead, Kentucky, as well as being selected as a finalist in the 7th International Poetry Contest sponsored by *Mattia*. She was recently awarded first prize in *The Heartland Review*'s short-short fiction contest. Thomas works on staff at a local newspaper and for an online magazine, and she currently teaches reading and writing at the middle school and college level. About her poem in this anthology, "Sacred Waters," Thomas writes: "The first time for such an event is never really forgotten but wavers at the backs our memories with every other encounter we have. The moment is fleeting, barely a breath-long, but the memory lasts always."

Becky Thompson's books include *When the Center Is on Fire* (University of Texas Press 2008, co-author, Diane Harriford), *A Promise and a Way of Life* (University of Minnesota Press 2001), *Mothering Without a Compass* (University of Minnesota Press 2000), and *A Hunger So Wide and So Deep* (University of Minnesota Press 1994). She is also co-editor of *Fingernails Across the Chalkboard: Poetry and Prose on HIV/AIDS From the Black Diaspora* with Randall Horton and Michael Hunter (Third World Press 2007). She teaches Sociology and African American Studies at Simmons College in Boston. Her recent poems have appeared in *The Harvard Review, We Begin Here: For Palestine and Lebanon, Warpland: A Journal of Black Literature and Ideas, Illuminations: An International Magazine of Contemporary Writing, My Soul Is Anchored: The Mourning Katrina National Writing Project,* and *The Teacher's Voice*. Of her poem in this anthology, "Post-Attica Visit," she writes: "The poem reflects my hope that my friend David Gilbert, political prisoner and social justice activist, be free, along with all other political prisoners in the world. Recovering our humanity will require making prisons obsolete."

Rhett Iseman Trull received her M.F.A. from the University of North Carolina at Greensboro, where she was a Randall Jarrell Fellow. Her poetry has appeared in many journals, including *Iron Horse Literary Review,*

Prairie Schooner, storySouth and *Zone 3*. She is the editor of *Cave Wall*. Of her poem in this anthology, "Counting Miracles at the State Asylum," she writes: "After years of struggling with manic depression and the sometimes necessary self-absorption that comes with it, I began to understand the healing power of awareness. In this poem, the characters find hope in the small but significant details of the world around them and their role in it, in this life that continues on and includes them. I guess this is what I try to do when I get caught up in the cycle of my moods. It's a practice that cures nothing, but somehow makes it easier to get through one moment and into the next."

Brian Turner earned an M.F.A. from the University of Oregon and lived abroad in South Korea for a year before serving for seven years in the U.S. Army. He was an infantry team leader for a year in Iraq beginning November 2003, with the 3rd Styker Brigade Combat Team, 2nd Infantry Division. Prior to that, he deployed to Bosnia-Herzegovina in 1999-2000 with the 10th Mountain Division. His poetry has been published in *Poetry Daily*, *The Georgia Review*, and other journals, and in the *Voices in Wartime Anthology* (Whit Press 2005) published in conjunction with the feature-length documentary film of the same name. His collection of poems about the Iraq War, *Here, Bullet* (Alice James Books 2005), won the 2005 Beatrice Hawley Award of Alice James Books. He received a 2007 NEA Literature Fellowship in Poetry. He currently lives in California.

Susan Varon is a poet and artist, recently relocated to Taos, New Mexico after living for 40 years in New York City. She began writing poetry in 1992, after suffering a severe stroke. Her work has appeared in more than 50 publications, and she has won fellowships to The MacDowell Colony and other residencies. She was ordained an Interfaith Minister in June 2005.

Pramila Venkateswaran, author of *Thirtha* (Yuganta Press 2002), has poems in *Paterson Literary Review*, *Ariel*, *Atlanta Review*, *Prairie Schooner*, *Kavya Bharati*, and *Calyx*, including anthologies *A Chorus for Peace: A Global Anthology of Women*, edited by Marilyn Arnold, Bonnie Baliff-Spanvill, and Kristen Tracy (University of Iowa Press, 2002), and *En(Compass)*, edited by Usha Akella (Yuganta Press 2004). She has performed her poems nationally, most recently in the Geraldine R. Dodge Poetry Festival. She is currently engaged in doing multimedia performances that include dance, poetry, and music. She teaches English and women's studies at Nassau Community College, New York. Of her poem in this anthology, "Praying for Miracles at Velankani Amman's Shrine, Tamil Nadu," she writes: "I wish to convey to people that faith in the goddess-as-healer is something ancient and continues to make us turn toward it in the acuteness of our physical and emotional pain. Describing the process of healing was important to me as a way to remember the experience and record it for family members who witnessed my suffering."

Ellen Doré Watson is director of The Poetry Center at Smith College, Northampton, Massachusetts. She teaches private writing workshops and serves as an editor of *The Massachusetts Review*. Author of three collections of poetry—including *Ladder Music* (Alice James Books 2001), which won the New York/New England Award from Alice James Books, *We Live in Bodies* (Alice James Books 1997) and *This Sharpening* (Tupelo Press 2006) —Watson was hailed by Library Journal as one of "24 poets for the 21st Century" and has been a recipient of a Massachusetts Cultural Council Artists Grant and a Rona Jaffe Writers' Award. Watson has also translated a dozen books from Brazilian Portuguese, including *The Alphabet in the Park* (Wesleyan 1990), the selected poems of Adelia Prado, for which Watson was awarded a National Endowment Translation Fellowship.

Afaa Michael Weaver's latest collection of poems is *The Plum Flower Dance* (University of Pittsburgh Press 2007). He has published eight previous collections of poetry. He has been a Pew fellow, a Fulbright Scholar, a Pushcart Prize winner, and is an Elder of Cave Canem. He studies Chinese and translates contemporary Chinese poetry. Weaver holds an M.A. in creative writing from Brown University and is Alumnae Professor of English at Simmons College in Boston, Massachusetts. According to *Poets &Writers* magazine, his son, Michael Shan Weaver, Jr., was born in 1971 with Down syndrome and died of complications at the age of 10 months; in 1995, Weaver was diagnosed with congestive heart failure and given five years to live, but through diet and medications, recovered sufficiently to be removed from the heart transplantation waiting list; Weaver has also struggled with depression and post-traumatic stress disorder resulting from his being an incest survivor. In the *Poets & Writers* article, which featured Weaver on its cover in the November/ December 2007 issue, he says, "Sometimes I wonder how I have not only survived but managed to produce a body of work that is ongoing. It feels like a miracle sometimes." In the same article, he attributed his ongoing recovery to being a Daoist and to the intense practice of Tai Ji Quan and Xing Yi Quan, which, he says, gives him "the strength of mind and spirit to deal with the challenge of recovering."

Patricia Wellingham-Jones, three-time Pushcart Prize nominee, has work published in numerous anthologies, journals and Internet magazines, including *HazMat Review*, *Poetry Depth Quarterly*, *Centrifugal Eye*, *Phoebe*, *A Room of Her Own*, *Pudding*, *Red River Review*, *Rattlesnake Review*, and *Ibbetson Street Press*. Her chapbook *End-Cycle: Poems About Caregiving* won the the Palabra Productions Chapbook Contest.

Marjory Heath Wentworth's poems have appeared in numerous books and magazines, and she has been nominated for the Pushcart Prize three times. Her collections of poetry include *Noticing Eden* (Hub City Writers Project 2003) and *Despite Gravity* (Ninety-Six Press 2007). She is the poet laureate of South Carolina. Of her poem in this anthology, "Linthong," Wentworth writes: "This poem is one Laotian refugee boy's survival story. I worked in the field of refugee resettlement for years in Geneva, Boston, and New York. All of the details in this poem come from that experience— from meeting refugees at airports to doing home visits when everyone had moved into one living space even though far more were provided, and people thought electrical wires were used for tying back hair, etc. Many Indochinese refugees had never seen running water or electricity before they arrived in the United States. Hmong refugees had no experience with a written language. Children, of course, always fared better than older people. They learned the language and ways of their adopted country with ease."

Meir Wieseltier, the most acclaimed Israeli poet in the generation after Yehuda Amichai, was born in Moscow in 1941 and moved to Israel in 1949. He has published 12 collections of poetry in Hebrew and translated the work of William Shakespeare, Charles Dickens, and Virginia Woolf, among others. He has received a number of literary awards, including the Prime Minister's Prize for Literature, the Bialik Prize, and Israel's most prestigious achievement award, the Israel Prize.

Janet Winans was born and raised in San Francisco, received her B.A. from Antioch College in Yellow Springs, Ohio. She lived in northern California for a number of years, married, had three children. She worked variously as co-director of a private school and summer camp, teacher, librarian, bookmobile driver and book salesperson. She wrote poetry during all those years. In the early 1980s, she divorced, left California for Arizona, and remarried. She received an M.F.A. in Poetry from the Warren Wilson Program for Writers, and for the next ten years, worked as a Poet in the Schools for the Arizona Commission on the Arts. She has continued to teach in community colleges and as a visiting poet in schools and libraries. She lives in Patagonia, Arizona. Of her poem in this anthology, "In Tule Fog," she writes: "Poetry writing is a vital component for me in terms of recovery. I need to put feelings into words on paper in order to make sense of my life and my place in the world. When these words resonate with others, we are all the better for it."

Terri Wolfe received her M.F.A. from Queens University of Charlotte in 2003 and currently teaches creative writing in that institution's Center for Lifelong Learning. Her poetry has appeared in *Iodine Poetry Journal*, *Wild Goose Poetry Review, Main Street Rag, Independence Boulevard*, and in *The Charlotte Writers' Club Anthology, Volume 3*. Of her poem in this anthology, "Timbuktu," Wolfe writes: "When my 27-year-old son took his life, I found myself in an alien landscape where nothing made sense. The depth of grief and the confusion I experienced cried out for acknowledgment, cried out for validation. When I began writing 'Timbuktu,' I think I wanted simply to chronicle the way in which our family chose to commemorate passing the milestone of the first anniversary of Jamie's death, but somewhere in the process I realized that the old cliché is true and if we choose, life does go on. It's a fragile existence, fraught with danger, but worth living if we have faith. I know that healing goes forward with writing about grief."

Diana Woodcock, assistant professor of English at Virginia Commonwealth University School of the Arts in Qatar, spent nearly eight years teaching in Tibet and Macau and working with Cambodian and Vietnamese refugees in camps on the Thai-Cambodian border. In 2007 she won the Creekwalker Prize for Poetry, was an Honorable Mention for the Robert G. Cohn Prose Poetry Award, and was a Finalist in Litchfield Review's poetry contest. She also was awarded a Summer Literary Seminars/Russia Select Scholarship as a finalist in their poetry competition. In 2006 she received an Honorable Mention in the *Nimrod/ Hardman Pablo Neruda Prize in Poetry Competition* and was an International Publication Prize winner in *Atlanta Review*'s Poetry Competition. She's been awarded residencies at Vermont Studio Center, Virginia Center for the Creative Arts, and the Everglades National Park. Her poems have appeared or are forthcoming in *Nimrod, Atlanta Review, Wisconsin Review, Hawaii Pacific Review, Litchfield Review, Brooklyn Review, Whiskey Island, Istanbul Literature Review, Blue Fifth Review, Hobble Creek Review, Quercus Review, Drumvoices Revue, Creekwalker* and other journals, as well as in anthologies such as *Susan B & Me* (Big Kids Publishing 2006), *Least-loved Beasts of the Really Wild West* (Native West Press 1997), and *Frontier: Custom and Archetype*. She has also taught English as a Second Language courses, and English as a Foreign Language courses in Tibet, Macau and Thailand.

Kevin Young's most recent collection is *For the Confederate Dead* (Alfred A. Knopf 2007), from which the title poem was reprinted in this anthology. He is the author of four previous collections of poetry and the editor of the Library of America's *John Berryman: Selected Poems* (2004), Everyman's Library Pocket Poets anthologies *Blues Poems* (2003) and *Jazz Poems* (2006), and *Giant Steps: The New Generation of African American Writers* (Harper Perennial 2000). His book *Jelly Roll* (Alfred A. Knopf 2005) was

375

a finalist for the National Book Award and the *Los Angeles Times* Book Prize, and won the Paterson Poetry Prize. The recent recipient of a Guggenheim fellowship and an NEA fellowship, Young is currently the Atticus Haygood Professor of English and Creative Writing and curator of the Raymond Danowski Poetry Library at Emory University in Atlanta, Georgia.

Index by Author's Name

Editing Notes

Readers may notice what appear to be stylistic inconsistencies among the poems in this anthology. Rather than imposing an external style on all poems for consistency, I have adhered to the original poem's internal style and to the poet's spellings and syntaxes. For example, readers may note spelling variations, such as "color" and "colour," may note group nouns with plural verbs, e.g., "the nation have...", and may note variations in the lengths of dashes used among the poems. At times, punctuation may seem irregular. Some poets have capitalized the first word in each line, some have not. In all cases, I have adhered to the spelling, syntax, punctuation, and stanza numbering of the poem as it appeared in its original publication. For previously unpublished poems, I have adhered to the style that the poet used in submission, after personal consultation with poets to clarify any editorial questions I posed.

Likewise, the form of poem titles are exactly as they appear in their original publications. For untitled poems, I have used brackets around the first line. Two of Rachel Tzvia Back's poems have titles using parentheses and italics, and I have kept that form for this anthology. I gave nearly all poets in this anthology the opportunity to write a few words about what their poems meant to them in terms of recovery. Some poets declined. A few did not respond. For those who agreed, I appended their words to the ends of their bios. In limited cases, I appended information gathered from other sources.

Tom Lombardo
Editor, *After Shocks: The Poetry of Recover for Life-Shattering Events*